THE CERTIFICATE OF PROFESSIONAL COMPETENCE

1001 TYPICAL QUESTIONS & ANSWERS

FOR THE ROAD GOODS NATIONAL AND INTERNATIONAL EXAMINATIONS

Plus 100 Typical Module A and B Questions and Answers for Northern Ireland Examinations

DAVID LOWE

KOGAN PAGE

First published in 1990 by
Kogan Page Ltd,
120 Pentonville Rd, London N1 9JN

British Library Cataloguing in Publication Data

A CIP catalogue record for this book is available from the British Library

ISBN 0-7494-0176-1

Typeset by Saxon Printing Ltd, Derby
Printed and bound in Great Britain by
Biddles Ltd, Guildford and King's Lynn

Contents

Introduction

The legal requirement for professional competence was introduced in the UK (at the instigation of the EC) on 1 January 1978 as a condition under which a standard operator's licence would be granted to permit the carriage of goods for hire or reward in either national or both national and international transport operations. Provisions in the regulations originally enabled certain people engaged in the road transport industry at that time to claim their 'professional competence' on the grounds of qualifying experience by obtaining a 'Grandfather Rights' Certificate of Professional Competence (CPC). Individuals who did not qualify under this scheme (which ended on 31 December 1979) may satisfy the requirements by holding membership, at specified grades, of one of the professional transport institutes. For those who do not qualify by these methods, however, and for young people entering the industry in future years, an examination system has been established which provides the professional competence qualification.

The collection of typical CPC questions in this book is intended to help those people taking the official examinations who need or want to acquire the professional competence qualification in order to take up positions in transport. Its purpose is to provide readers with a means of revision and self-testing of the knowledge required for both the national – module A (which applies to both goods and PSV operations) and module B (goods only) and the Northern Ireland version – and the international examinations in road goods transport and to familiarise them with the type of questions set in the examinations. It should help candidates to study privately, at home and elsewhere, when just a few spare moments are available for revision or when it is convenient to devote longer periods to study. The questions selected are known to be typical for the examinations. A number of them have actually appeared in Royal Society of Arts sample question papers (and acknowledgement is given for reproducing these in this book) while many others have featured in past examinations. Yet another part of the collection is of 'made up' questions but nevertheless these again are typical of both the type of question found in the examination and the subject material used as a basis for devising official questions. Answers are provided for all the questions at the end of the book.

To help potential examinees, the text also includes information on the legal requirements for professional competence and on the examination system, as well as giving details of the current official Royal Society of Arts syllabuses for Great Britain and Northern Ireland. Readers will see that the syllabus covers a broad range of subjects – from matters directly concerning the legal and administrative aspects of goods vehicle operation to technical aspects of vehicle construction and use, maintenance and road safety measures. It also covers the much wider issues of business management such as administration, financial control, knowledge of the law and the structure of business plus the complexities of social legislation. The typical questions included in the book reflect this broad range of subjects.

Acknowledgement

I am grateful for the use of many questions published by the Royal Society of Arts in its typical examination papers both for my Professional Competence Study Manual (published by Kogan Page, London) and for this book. I also make acknowledgement to the RSA in regard to the publication here of its official examination syllabus.

1: Requirement for professional competence

The Goods Vehicles (Operators' Licences, Qualifications and Fees) Regulations 1984 (SI 1984/176) (as amended SI 1986/666, SI 1986/1391 and SI 1987/841 - available from HMSO) require that individuals or transport firms who wish to engage in the carriage of goods by road for hire or reward and, consequently, hold a standard operator's licence, must satisfy conditions of professional competence, either with the operator himself holding the qualification or by the employment of a person (on a full-time basis) who is professionally competent. A person in this position who did not qualify under the original 'Grandfather Rights' provisions mentioned earlier, or who is not exempt on the basis of institute membership, must pass the official Royal Society of Arts examination in order to qualify for professional competence.

Transfer of professional competence qualification

Those who qualify for professional competence in Great Britain can transfer their qualification to Northern Ireland or to any other member state of the European Community (ie France, West Germany, Italy, Netherlands, Belgium, Luxemburg, Denmark, Eire, Spain, Portugal and Greece) to enable them to operate a road haulage business or obtain a position as a transport manager in a haulage business in any of those countries. A 'Certificate of Qualification' confirming this can be obtained by applying to a Licensing Authority and paying the appropriate fee.

2: The RSA syllabus - GB and NI

A study syllabus covering the professional competence examination subjects is available from the Royal Society of Arts. Study may be undertaken at courses organised by a number of bodies including the Road Transport Industry Training Board (RTITB), group training associations, trade associations or commercial organisations. Some local technical colleges and other teaching establishments also offer part-time (usually evening), classes on the subject. The study may involve full-time or part-time attendance at such courses or it may be by correspondence course, with a home learning package (ie notes and cassette tapes) or with the aid of teaching manuals. The author's *A Study Manual of Professional Competence in Road Transport Management* (7th edition, published September 1989 by Kogan Page, London) has been used successfully by many examination candidates without resorting to attendance at study courses or evening classes.

Length of Study Course

The Royal Society of Arts recommends that study for the national examination should involve some 72 hours of direct teaching, and for the international examination a further 30 hours of teaching. Examination candidates starting with no prior knowledge whatsoever of either transport operations or the ways of business, and particularly those without any assisted tuition, may find that they need considerably more time than this, which in any case does not include time needed for private study outside the tuition periods.

The syllabus

The published RSA syllabus for goods transport operations is detailed here:

Syllabus for the Goods National Examination (modules A and B)

A: Road Safety

1. **Drivers' hours and records**
   - **1.1 Basic hours requirements**
   - **1.2 Hours of work records (record sheets)**
   - **1.3 Hours of work records (tachographs)**
2. **HGV driving licences**
3. **General traffic regulations**
   - ***3.1 Speed limits***
   - ***3.2 Parking, waiting, loading and unloading***
   - ***3.3 Traffic offences and legal action***
4. **Procedure in case of traffic accidents**
5. **Vehicle, goods and passenger liability insurance**
6. **Safe loading of vehicles and transit of goods**

B: Technical Standards and Aspects of Operation

1. **Weights and dimensions of vehicles**
   - **1.1 Vehicle weights**
   - **1.2 Axle weights**
   - **1.3 Maximum dimensions of the vehicle**
2. **Vehicle selection**
   - **2.1 Definition of different types of vehicle and their suitability**
3. **Mechanical conditions**
   - **3.1 Plating and testing**
   - **3.2 Construction and Use regulations**
   - **3.3 Lighting and marking**
   - **3.4 Operator's responsibility in relation to maintenance records and standards**
   - **3.5 Fleet inspection and roadside checks**

C: Access to the GB Market

1. **Licensing**
   - **1.1 The system of 'O' licensing - in particular the role of the Licensing Authority**

D: Business and Financial Management

1. **Financial management**
   - ***1.1 Sources and uses of funds***

- *1.2 The purpose of accounts and balance sheet and management information derived from accounting*
- *1.3 Capital*
- *1.4 Cash flow*
- *1.5 Purchasing and stock control*

2. **Commercial conduct of the business**
   - **2.1 Vehicle costing**
   - **2.2 Methods of payment and collection of revenue**
   - *2.3 Documents and records involved in commercial practice*
   - *2.4 Banking and similar services*
3. **General insurance**
   - *3.1 Advantages and scope of insurance*
4. **Methods of operating**

E: Law

1. **Structure of law**
   - *1.1 Law of business and carriage*
   - *1.2 Operator's and employee's liability for civil and criminal acts*
2. **Business and company law**
   - *2.1 The formation and legal function of a business*
3. **Social legislation**
   - *3.1 Industrial relations*
   - *3.2 Social security*
   - *3.3 Discrimination*
   - *3.4 Safety*
4. **Taxation**
   - **4.1 Vehicle excise duty and registration**
   - **4.2 Trade licences (plates)**

NB: *Items shown in italic typeface above (as this NB) comprise those examined in module A which apply to both goods and PSV operations. The remainder comprise subjects covered by the module B examination which apply to goods vehicle operations only.*

Syllabus for the Goods International Examination (module D)

A: Law

1. **Hours and conditions of work and records**
   - **1.1 The AETR Agreement**
   - **1.2 Tachographs**

B: Access to the Market

1. **Bilateral Agreements**

2. **Multilateral Agreements**
3. **Tariffs**
4. **Other documentation required**
5. **Fiscal charges**

C: Customs, Practice and Formalities

1. **Customs procedures**
   - 1.1 **General procedures**
   - 1.2 **Community transit/carnets**
   - 1.3 **Carnets**
   - 1.4 **Other Customs documentation**
2. **Insurance and carrier's liability**
3. **Financial aspects**

D: Operations, Technical Standards and Road Safety

1. **Route planning**
2. **Vehicle construction, weights and dimensions and safety**
3. **Laws, regulations and administrative provisions applicable to traffic within the Community**
4. **Other forms of transport operations.**

Syllabus for the Goods National (Northern Ireland) Examination

A: Road Safety

1. **Driver's hours and records**
   - 1.1 **Basic hours requirements**
   - 1.2 **Hours of work records**
2. **HGV driving licences**
3. **General Traffic Regulations**
   - 3.1 **Speed limits**
   - 3.2 **Parking, waiting, loading and unloading**
   - 3.3 **Traffic offences and legal action**
4. **Procedure in the case of traffic accidents**
5. **Compulsory Vehicle and passenger insurance**
6. **Safe loading of vehicles and transit of goods**

B: Technical Standards and Aspects of Operation

1. **Weights and dimensions of vehicles**
   - 1.1 **Vehicle weights**
   - 1.2 **Axle weights**
   - 1.3 **Maximum dimensions of the vehicle**
2. **Vehicle selection**
   - 2.1 **Definition of different types of vehicle and their suitability**

3. **Mechanical conditions**
   - **3.1 Construction and Use regulations**
   - **3.2 Goods vehicle certification**
   - **3.3 Lighting and marking**
   - **3.4 Operator's responsibility in relation to maintenance records and standards**
   - **3.5 Roadside checks**

C: Access to the Northern Ireland Market

1. **Licensing**
   - **1.1 Licences**
   - **1.2 Admission to the occupation**

D: Business and Financial Management

1. **Financial Management**
   - **1.1 Sources and uses of funds**
   - **1.2 The purpose of accounts and balance sheets and management information derived from accounting**
   - **1.3 Capital**
   - **1.4 Cash flow**
   - **1.5 Purchasing and stock control**
2. **Commercial conduct of the business**
   - **2.1 Vehicle costing**
   - **2.2 Method of payment and collection of revenue**
   - **2.3 Documents and records involved in commercial practice**
   - **2.4 Banking services**
3. **Other services**
   - **3.1 Advantages and scope of insurance**
   - **3.2 Methods of operating**

E: Law

1. **Structure of law**
   - **1.1 Law of business and carriage**
   - **1.2 Operator's and employee's liability for civil and criminal acts**
2. **Company law**
   - **2.1 The formation and legal functions of a business**
3. **Social Legislation**
   - **3.1 Industrial relations**
   - **3.2 Social security**
   - **3.3 Discrimination**
   - **3.4 Safety**

4. Taxation
   4.1 Vehicle excise duty and registration
   4.2 Trade licences

NB: ***For Northern Ireland candidates the international examination is identical to that conducted at centres on the British mainland.***

Examination candidates should note that the RSA has stated that examination questions will be based on the syllabus 'as published' (see above). Where current legislation is changed, the content will not be examined for at least three months from the date of implementation. Where current legislation remains unchanged in detail, yet becomes embodied within new legislation, the content will continue to be examined. Legislation which has been repealed or revoked will not be examined.

Those wishing to study for the examination should ensure that they have an up-to-date syllabus (either GB or NI as appropriate), which covers both goods and passenger vehicle operations, available from the Royal Society of Arts, Examinations Department, Murray Road, Orpington, Kent BR5 3RB (tel: 0689 32421).

3: The official examination

Examinations for professional competence in road transport are conducted at centres throughout the country on behalf of the official examining body, the Royal Society of Arts. Normally, examinations are held four times a year (three times only in NI) usually in March, June, October (except NI) and December on dates which are published by the RSA. A list of examination centres and future dates can be obtained from the RSA.

On the day of the examinations, the 'core' examination (module A) and the national examination (module B) are held in the morning. The module A examination taken by both road freight and road passenger candidates lasts for 30 minutes and comprises 20 questions. The subject material on which the core examination is based is shown in the official syllabus in *italic typeface*. After a 15-minute interval the separate freight (module B) and passenger (module C) national examinations are held. These last for one hour and comprise 40 questions. The international examination (module D for freight and module E for passenger candidates) is held later that day so that candidates can sit all three modules on the same day at the same location if they so wish (and provided the examination centre has sufficient entries to run all sections). The international examination lasts for one hour and comprises 30 questions.

Candidates who pass either the module A or module B parts of the examination will be granted a 'credit' until such time as they pass the remaining part; they will then be fully qualified as professionally competent in national road freight or road passenger operations (the two individual A and B credit certificates can be exchanged for a combined certificate on application to the RSA). Each part of the examination can be taken and paid for separately, but where a candidate sits all three parts on the same day at the same location, a reduced combined fee is charged.

Fees for the examinations in 1990 are as follows:

1. Module A (core) £5.00 if taken separately
2. Module B (freight) and C (PSV) £9.20 if taken separately
3. Modules A and B (national) or A and C (PSV national) £13.60 if taken together
4. Module D (international) or E (PSV international) £13.00
5. Modules A, B and D (freight) or A, C and E (PSV) taken on the same day £21.50.

Additional local administrative fees will be charged by examination centres.

Unsuccessful examination candidates may apply for details of their performance. An application form (obtainable from the RSA) should be sent with a fee of £2.50 in respect of each examination failed.

Examination method

Examinations conducted for the purpose of providing the professional competence qualification are based on the 'objective testing' or multiple choice method. This means that the candidate is faced either with a number of questions, each of which is provided with a choice of possible answers (usually four), only one of which is correct, or alternatively with statements of fact to which a 'True' or 'False' answer must be given. Candidates must select, and mark on the answer paper, what they believe to be the correct answer to each question or statement.

With this method of examination, the need for high standards of literacy is removed and it ensures uniform standards of marking for all candidates. The examinations are designed to be within the grasp of candidates whose educational standard corresponds to the level normally reached at school-leaving age.

The typical questions included in this selection reflect the subjects regularly featured in recent examinations. Where two or more questions in the following pages appear to raise or answer the same point, or merely appear to be the same words turned round, this is done deliberately in order to give candidates maximum experience in answering likely questions in the various alternative ways in which the examiners may set them. Further, for those sections of the syllabus which cause particular difficulty for candidates, such as financial matters, law and industrial relations, a greater proportion of typical questions are included to help examinees to prepare themselves. Answering the questions in this book will undoubtedly add to the candidate's knowledge of syllabus subjects and if they can be answered without checking the answers beforehand then the odds are that success in the examination will be achieved.

Candidates are advised to read the examination questions *very carefully*. While the examination does not feature 'trick' questions, the examiners do endeavour to set questions with a degree of difficulty to test the candidate's knowledge and intelligence to the full. Thus some questions are not quite as straightforward as they may seem at first glance. The author recommends candidates to read each question very carefully and then to ask themselves, 'what am I being asked here ?'. When they are sure they know what the question is really asking, then - and only then - should they look to see what choice of answers are given. Where examinees are not sure they know the correct answer to a question, they should consider each given answer in turn and determine whether each could possibly be right. Often two out of the four choices are very wide of the mark and can easily be discounted. This reduces the odds quite considerably for guessing the right answer. Many candidates come out of the examination room kicking themselves because they quickly realise, when it is too late, that they did not read a question carefully enough or properly interpret what they were being asked.

Suggestions for use of this book

1. Cover up the questions ahead of the one you are currently thinking about because subsequent questions may give clues to the correct answers to earlier ones.
2. Do not mark answers in the book: use a separate sheet of paper for this purpose to allow for repeated use of the book.
3. Finally: *Read the questions very carefully*. Best of luck.

4: Typical Questions – National Examination Module A: Goods and PSV Syllabus

A1 Speed Limits

1. A 'restricted' road is a road in a built-up area where, usually, a 30mph speed limit applies and where the street lamps are not more than:

   (a) 100 feet apart
   (b) 100 yards apart
   (c) 200 feet apart
   (d) 200 yards apart

2. Vehicles used by the emergency services are exempt from speed limits at all times.

   (a) True
   (b) False

3. When a vehicle subject to a specific speed limit is driven on a section of road where a different speed limit applies, the maximum speed at which it should be driven is:

   (a) the lower limit applicable to the vehicle
   (b) the lower limit applicable to the road
   (c) the higher limit applicable to the vehicle
   (d) the lower limit applicable to either the road or the vehicle

4. The general speed limit on de-restricted roads other than motorways and dual-carriageway roads is:

   (a) 40mph
   (b) 50mph
   (c) 60mph

(d) 70mph

5. **Unless a lower speed limit applies, the maximum speed permitted for a motor vehicle on a dual carriageway is:**

(a) 70mph
(b) 60mph
(c) 50mph
(d) 40mph

A2 Parking, Waiting, Loading etc.

6. **On roads sign-posted as rural clearways, restrictions on stopping do not apply to goods vehicles loading or unloading.**

(a) True
(b) False

7. **On roads sign-posted as rural clearways waiting restrictions apply for:**

(a) 4 hours daily
(b) 8 hours daily
(c) 12 hours daily
(d) 24 hours daily

8. **On roads sign-posted as urban clearways stopping restrictions apply only:**

(a) during morning and evening peak periods
(b) from 7.00am to 7.00pm on Mondays to Fridays only
(c) for 24 hours every day
(d) from 7.00am to 7.00pm every day

9. **Drivers are prohibited from stopping in a zebra crossing controlled area for which of the following reasons?**

(a) to avoid an accident
(b) to give precedence to a pedestrian on the crossing
(c) to load or unload goods
(d) to make a right or left turn

10. **A vehicle has precedence over pedestrians at a pelican crossing when the amber light is flashing.**

    (a) True
    (b) False

11. **Goods vehicles may stop in vacant parking meter bays, without payment, to load and unload for up to:**

    (a) 10 minutes
    (b) 15 minutes
    (c) 20 minutes
    (d) 30 minutes

12. **A driver who parks his vehicle on a pavement or roadside verge to load or unload commits an offence if:**

    (a) it is parked with the prior permission of a police officer
    (b) it is left with the hazard warning flashers operating
    (c) the loading/unloading could not have been reasonably carried out otherwise
    (d) it is more than 7.5 tonnes maximum permissible weight

13. **Goods vehicles not exceeding 1,525kg unladen weight can be parked without lights at night, provided they are in a 30mph speed limit area, are parked on the nearside of the road and not within:**

    (a) 15 feet from a road junction
    (b) 10 metres from a road junction on either side
    (c) 10 yards from a road junction on either side
    (d) 15 yards from a road junction

14. **A driver is prohibited from stopping his vehicle on the hard shoulder of a motorway:**

    (a) when he is taken ill
    (b) to give assistance to another vehicle which has broken down
    (c) to allow him to take an official break
    (d) in the case of an accident

15. **Vehicles with an operating weight exceeding 7.5 tonnes are allowed to use the right-hand lane of motorways:**

(a) only in exceptional circumstances
(b) under no circumstances whatsoever
(c) at any time when it is safe to do so
(d) to pass another vehicle carrying a wide load

16. Rural clearways are indicated by signs comprising:

(a) a circular plate with red border and diagonal cross on a blue background
(b) a rectangular plate with black lettering on a yellow background
(c) a circular plate with a white symbol on a blue background
(d) an octagonal plate with white letters on a red background

17. On a road marked as an urban clearway, stopping is prohibited at specified times except for picking up or setting down passengers when the stop may last for up to:

(a) one minute
(b) two minutes
(c) four minutes
(d) five minutes

18. A circular road sign bordered in red and showing a black silhouette of a vehicle and the symbol '7.5 T' means that goods vehicles:

(a) exceeding 7.5 tonnes unladen may pass
(b) exceeding 7.5 tonnes gross weight are prohibited
(c) not exceeding 7.5 tonnes unladen may pass
(d) not exceeding 7.5 tonnes gross weight are prohibited

19. A single continuous yellow line painted on the road parallel to the kerb means:

(a) waiting is prohibited at peak hours
(b) waiting is prohibited at any time
(c) waiting is prohibited for at least 8 hours during the working day
(d) waiting is prohibited at any time during the working day

20. **A single broken yellow line painted on the road parallel to the kerb means:**
    (a) loading/unloading is prohibited during every working day
    (b) loading/unloading is prohibited at any other times as shown on the nearby sign
    (c) waiting is prohibited during every working day
    (d) waiting is prohibited during any other period as shown on the nearby sign

21. **A waiting prohibition that applies during every working day is indicated on a sign which shows the days and times when the restriction applies, and is further indicated by:**
    (a) a single continuous yellow line painted parallel to the kerb
    (b) a single broken yellow line painted parallel to the kerb
    (c) a double yellow line painted parallel to the kerb
    (d) double yellow lines painted on the kerb at right angles to the road

22. **A single yellow line painted on the kerb edging at right angles to the road means:**
    (a) waiting is prohibited during every working day
    (b) waiting is prohibited during any other periods
    (c) loading/unloading is prohibited during every working day
    (d) loading/unloading is prohibited during any other period

23. **A double yellow line painted on the kerb edging at right angles to the road means that loading and unloading is prohibited:**
    (a) during every working day
    (b) during peak hours on working days only
    (c) during 24 hours every day
    (d) during the hours of darkness only

24. **Three yellow lines painted on the kerb edging at right angles to the road means:**

(a) loading/unloading is prohibited during every working day
(b) loading/unloading is prohibited during every working day and at other times
(c) loading/unloading is prohibited at peak times on working days
(d) waiting is prohibited during the working day and at other times

25. It is illegal for vehicles other than PSVs to use bus lanes:

(a) only on normal working days
(b) during morning and evening peak periods
(c) on any day when buses are operating
(d) during times when the lanes are in operation (as indicated on a nearby sign)

26. Although no restrictions on loading and unloading are signposted, a police constable may still direct a driver to move his vehicle if it causes an obstruction:

(a) True
(b) False

27. A police constable in uniform or a vehicle examiner can direct a driver of a goods vehicle to take it to a place for inspection or weighing without risk of a claim for expenses, providing the distance does not exceed:

(a) 3 miles
(b) 4 miles
(c) 5 miles
(d) 10 miles

28. Traffic wardens are appointed by:

(a) the area Licensing Authority
(b) the local authority
(c) the local police authority
(d) the Secretary of State for Transport

29. Which of the following offences are not within a traffic warden's power to take action?

(a) driving without a current or valid driving licence
(b) causing an obstruction or contravening waiting restrictions
(c) parking a vehicle at night without lights
(d) failing to display a current vehicle excise licence disc

30. Persons employed as parking attendants by the local highway authority have duties in connection with:

(a) school crossing patrols
(b) the use of parking bays
(c) the fixed penalty system
(d) point duties for traffic control

31. If a traffic warden believes a person to be the driver of a vehicle which is illegally parked without lights, he has the power to require that person to:

(a) provide his name and address
(b) produce his driving licence
(c) produce a test certificate for the vehicle
(d) produce evidence of insurance for the vehicle

32. Traffic wardens have power to enforce the law in connection with offences concerning:

(a) stealing motor vehicles
(b) failing to stop following a road accident
(c) driving a vehicle with defective tyres
(d) leaving a vehicle parked at night without lights

33. Excess parking charges are normally payable within:

(a) 14 days of the issue of the notice
(b) 21 days of the issue of the notice
(c) 28 days of the issue of the notice
(d) the time period stated in the notice

34. Under the fixed penalty system, if the offending driver does not elect to have the case dealt with by a court, he must pay the penalty within:

(a) 7 days
(b) 14 days

(c) 21 days
(d) 28 days

35. If a fixed penalty has not been paid within the statutory period, within what period of time must the police contact the registered keeper of the vehicle for a statutory statement of ownership?

(a) 21 days
(b) 3 months
(c) 4 months
(d) 6 months

A3 Traffic Offences

36. Which of the following offences, on conviction by a court, will result in automatic endorsement of a driving licence?

(a) using a vehicle without a valid test certificate
(b) making a U-turn in a prohibited area
(c) using a vehicle without insurance against third party risks
(d) causing an obstruction with a vehicle

37. A driver convicted of three driving licence endorsable offences committed on the same occasion and which carry 3, 4 and 5 penalty points respectively will have which of the following number of points endorsed on his driving licence?

(a) 3 points
(b) 5 points
(c) 9 points
(d) 12 points

38. Where 12 penalty points for offences committed within a 3-year period have already been added to a licence and the driver has been disqualified once previously during that period, unless he can put forward mitigating circumstances acceptable to the court he will be disqualified for at least:

(a) 3 years

(b) 2 years
(c) 1 year
(d) 6 months

39. Which of the following motoring offences will result in discretionary driving licence disqualification on conviction?

(a) racing on the highway
(b) causing death by reckless driving
(c) failure to stop after an accident
(d) driving while under the influence of drink or drugs

40. Unless the court accepts a plea of exceptional hardship, a conviction for reckless driving will result in:

(a) obligatory disqualification
(b) discretionary disqualification
(c) endorsement of full penalty points
(d) endorsement of 8-10 penalty points

41. Which of the following offences requires the court to impose an obligatory disqualification from driving unless there are acceptable grounds of exceptional hardship?

(a) exceeding statutory speed limits
(b) reckless driving within three years of a similar conviction
(c) being in charge of a vehicle while having an excessive breath/alcohol level
(d) leaving a vehicle in a dangerous position

42. One of the offences which incurs obligatory disqualification of a driving licence on conviction is:

(a) driving with uncorrected defective eyesight
(b) failing to stop at a traffic signal
(c) exceeding the speed limit
(d) motor racing on the highway

43. Three of the offences listed below incur automatic disqualification from driving for a minimum of 12 months, unless the court accepts reasons of exceptional hardship. Which of the offences does not incur this penalty?

(a) causing death by reckless driving
(b) a second reckless driving offence in a 3-year period
(c) racing on a highway
(d) being in charge of a motor vehicle while under the influence of drink or drugs

44. The minimum period of mandatory driving licence disqualification for a second drink/driving offence committed within 10 years is:

(a) 10 years
(b) 11 years
(c) 3 years
(d) 5 years

45. A person who is disqualified from driving for more than 10 years may apply to the court to have his disqualification removed:

(a) after 2 years from the date on which it was imposed
(b) after half the period of disqualification has expired
(c) after 5 years from the date of disqualification
(d) at no time during the disqualification period

46. When an application for removal of a driving licence disqualification is refused by the court, the applicant may re-apply at intervals of:

(a) 1 month
(b) 2 months
(c) 3 months
(d) 6 months

47. For which of the following offences committed by a driver would the vehicle user also be liable to prosecution and a penalty of driving licence endorsement or disqualification?

(a) failing to comply with the conditions of a provisional licence
(b) stealing a motor vehicle

(c) use of a vehicle uninsured against third party risks
(d) illegally carrying a passenger on a motor cycle

48. If a driver is disqualified from driving, he must automatically surrender his HGV licence to the Licensing Authority.

(a) True
(b) False

49. A driving licence will be endorsed if the driver is convicted of which of the following offences?

(a) failing to comply with traffic directions
(b) driving without statutory lights
(c) sounding a horn during the hours of darkness
(d) failing to use the vehicle reversing alarm

50. Driving licence endorsements for driving with a breath/alcohol level above the statutory limit remain in force for:

(a) 3 years
(b) 4 years
(c) 10 years
(d) 11 years

51. Except in the case of certain drink/driving offences, a driving licence endorsement remains in force for a period of:

(a) 3 years
(b) 4 years
(c) 10 years
(d) 11 years

52. If a driving licence was endorsed for a drink/driving offence on 1 September 1989, the earliest date on which an application can be made for its removal is:

(a) 1 September 1990
(b) 1 September 1992
(c) 1 September 1999
(d) 1 September 2000

53. A police constable in uniform can request a driver to take a breath test at the roadside if he had reason to suspect the driver of having committed a traffic offence.

(a) True
(b) False

54. For the purposes of the breathalyser test, the prescribed limit for a driver is:

(a) 30 microgrammes of alcohol in 100 millilitres of breath
(b) 35 microgrammes of alcohol in 100 millilitres of breath
(c) 40 microgrammes of alcohol in 100 millilitres of breath
(d) 50 microgrammes of alcohol in 100 millilitres of breath

55. Where a driver is found by the police to have a breath/alcohol level of 30 microgrammes of alcohol per 100 millilitres of breath, he is over the statutory limit and has committed an offence:

(a) True
(b) False

56. It is an offence to drive a motor vehicle on the road when the level of alcohol in the breath exceeds:

(a) 20 microgrammes of alcohol per 80 millilitres of breath
(b) 25 microgrammes of alcohol per 100 millilitres of breath
(c) 35 microgrammes of alcohol per 100 millilitres of breath
(d) 50 microgrammes of alcohol per 150 millilitres of breath

57. A person is liable to be convicted of an offence of driving with an excessive blood/alcohol level when this exceeds:

(a) 70 milligrammes of alcohol in 120 millilitres of blood

(b) **80 milligrammes of alcohol in 100 millilitres of blood**
(c) **80 milligrammes of alcohol in 120 millilitres of blood**
(d) **100 milligrammes of alcohol in 80 millilitres of blood**

58. Where an employed driver is charged with not complying with vehicle insurance requirements, he has a valid defence if he can prove to the court that the vehicle did not belong to him and that he had no reason to believe it was not insured.

(a) **True**
(b) **False**

59. For which of the following offences could a goods vehicle operator be convicted by a court even though he was not driving the vehicle at the time?

(a) **failure of the driver to stop following an accident as required by law**
(b) **failure of the driver to comply with authorised traffic directions**
(c) **failure to hold insurance cover against third party risks**
(d) **failure of the driver to give his name at the scene of an accident**

60. The registered keeper of a vehicle would not be liable for payment of fixed penalty charges if he can prove that at the relevant time the vehicle was in the possession of another person without his consent.

(a) **True**
(b) **False**

61. Which of the following traffic offences can result in a fixed penalty?

(a) **driving while uninsured against third party risks**
(b) **driving carelessly**
(c) **causing damage to authorised traffic signs**
(d) **driving the wrong way in a one-way street**

62. A fixed penalty notice can be issued by a police constable or a traffic warden for the offence of:

(a) parking a vehicle on a road at night without lights
(b) careless driving
(c) driving when uninsured against third party risks
(d) failure to sign a driving licence

63. Under the driving licence penalty points system, the number of points incurred for exceeding the speed limit is:

(a) 3 points
(b) 4 points
(c) 5 to 8 points at the discretion of the court
(d) 9 points

A4 Responsibility for Maintenance

64. When a haulier contracts out his vehicle service and repairs, the legal responsibility for keeping maintenance records rests with:

(a) the operator
(b) both the operator and the repair garage
(c) neither the operator nor the repair garage
(d) the repair garage

65. A transport operator must keep records of all defect inspections and repairs to his 'O' licensed vehicles and preserve them for at least:

(a) 6 months
(b) 9 months
(c) 12 months
(d) 15 months

66. If a transport operator has a proper maintenance agreement with a repair garage, then so far as his 'O' licence is concerned, responsibility for an unroadworthy vehicle rests with the repairer.

(a) True
(b) False

67. **Goods Vehicle Licensing Authorities require operators to have their vehicle maintenance inspections carried out at intervals of:**

(a) once every month
(b) once every two months
(c) 3,000-5,000 miles
(d) no specified interval of time

A5 Financial Management

68. **How does a firm of 'factors' provide a company with funds?**

(a) by acting as a debt collection agency
(b) by buying a company's fixed assets and leasing them back
(c) by purchasing the company's debts for immediate cash
(d) by reducing the time limits given to customers in which to pay

69. **Where a firm which has an inadequate cash flow sells its invoices at less than their face value to a third party this is called:**

(a) provision for bad debts
(b) trade invoicing
(c) debt factoring
(d) debt collection

70. **Which of the following is an internal source of company funds?**

(a) reducing investment in stock
(b) offering preference shares to employees
(c) obtaining a bank overdraft
(d) making a share scrip issue

71. **The high street clearing banks offer which of the following types of funds?**

(a) long term capital investment
(b) debentures

(c) investment opportunities
(d) short-term financing facilities

72. Which of the following is a source of short-term financing for a typical road haulage company?

(a) a debenture issue
(b) an issue of ordinary shares
(c) retained profits of the company
(d) a bank overdraft

73. What is the main advantage of using hire purchase as a source of funds?

(a) the firm never actually owns the goods so does not have a progressively devaluing asset
(b) the length of loan period is usually long and interest rates are low
(c) essential equipment can be acquired with minimum capital outlay
(d) equipment acquired by this means can readily be disposed of if it becomes redundant

74. A firm needing to employ additional labour for a short-term contract, entailing an additional outlay of some £30,000, would most readily raise the extra funds:

(a) by seeking a bank overdraft
(b) by making a rights share issue
(c) by an additional share issue
(d) by raising a debenture

75. Which of the following methods would be the best way of financing increased stocks of raw materials?

(a) by hire purchase loan
(b) by leasing stock
(c) by reducing the credit given to customers
(d) by bank overdraft facility

76. Debentures issued as a source of funds would be described as:

(a) long-term loans
(b) ordinary share stock

(c) preference share stock
(d) retained profits

77. The long-term funds of a company would normally include:

(a) its bank overdraft
(b) its petty cash float
(c) the value of its debtor invoices
(d) the original capital invested when the company was started

78. A source of short-term funds for a business would be:

(a) a mortgage on premises
(b) the firm's share capital
(c) a bank overdraft facility
(d) capital invested by the founders of the firm

79. Ordinary shares issued by a limited company are considered to be:

(a) a source of long-term funds
(b) a source of short-term funds
(c) a long-term asset
(d) a short-term liability

80. Which of the following would be treated as short-term company funds?

(a) its ordinary shares
(b) its tax reserves
(c) its debenture stock
(d) the capital employed

81. Limited liability companies are required to pay their debenture holders annual interest on their loans:

(a) only if they can afford to do so
(b) even if trading losses have been made during the year
(c) if the shareholders agree that such interest should be paid
(d) on a voluntary basis but only if profits have been made

82. **A balance sheet is a statement of company affairs at a given date showing:**

(a) its annual sales and purchases
(b) its operating costs
(c) its detailed operating expenditure
(d) its assets and liabilities

83. **A company balance sheet is a statement of its financial position:**

(a) for the 13 four-weekly trading periods
(b) for the financial year
(c) for any fixed period
(d) at a given date

84. **The Companies Act requires a limited liability company to produce a balance sheet every:**

(a) 6 months
(b) 9 months
(c) 12 months
(d) 24 months

85. **Which company official is required to certify that the balance sheet of a company gives a true and accurate statement of the company's financial affairs?**

(a) the Registrar of Companies
(b) its officially appointed auditors
(c) one or all of the directors
(d) the company secretary

86. **The amount of a firm's capital may be determined by examining:**

(a) its trading account
(b) its annual balance sheet
(c) its profit and loss account
(d) its management accounts

87. **Which of the following financial calculations will determine the net worth of a company?**

(a) the value of its assets plus its liabilities

(b) the value of its assets multiplied by its liabilities
(c) the value of its assets less its liabilities
(d) the value of its assets divided by its liabilities

88. Which of the following items would not be found in a firm's profit and loss account?

(a) tax paid in the year
(b) the total amount of capital employed in the business
(c) annual depreciation on its fixed assets
(d) interest on any bank or other loans

89. Which of the following items would be expected to be shown in a firm's trading and profit and loss account?

(a) its total annual turnover
(b) amounts owing to creditors
(c) its bank overdraft at the year end
(d) the value of its unpaid debtors

90. Which of the following items would be reflected as a direct expense on a firm's trading and profit and loss account?

(a) local authority rates on premises
(b) anticipated benefits from advertising
(c) vehicle repairs
(d) additional share allocations

91. Increased wage payments to employees appear in company accounts as:

(a) increased expenditure in the balance sheet
(b) increased expenditure in the trading account
(c) reduced profit in the balance sheet
(d) decreased revenue in the profit and loss account

92. Which of the following ratios can be calculated from a firm's annual profit and loss account?

(a) annual turnover as a percentage of total capital employed
(b) gross profit as a percentage of annual turnover
(c) fixed capital as a percentage of total capital employed

(d) current ratio

93. If a firm's final accounts show profit as £25,000 on an annual turnover of £200,000, what is its profit margin?

(a) 10.0 per cent
(b) 12.5 per cent
(c) 13.5 per cent
(d) 20.0 per cent

94. Debentures carrying a mortgage on the firm's premises would appear in its balance sheet under the general heading of:

(a) current liabilities
(b) long-term liabilities
(c) ordinary shares
(d) share capital

95. Stocks of vehicle and heating fuel would be shown in a firm's balance sheet as:

(a) fixed assets
(b) current assets
(c) current liabilities
(d) long-term liabilities

96. Which of the following items would be shown as current assets in a company's balance sheet?

(a) amounts owing to creditors
(b) its current overdraft and any bank loans
(c) credit balances in its bank accounts and petty cash in hand
(d) dividends to be paid to shareholders

97. A debenture is shown in a company's balance sheet as:

(a) a current liability
(b) a floating liability
(c) a fixed asset
(d) a current asset

98. A financial statement of annual sales turnover, expenditure and net profit for a firm over a given period is called:

(a) an income and expenditure report
(b) a trading and profit and loss account
(c) the balance sheet
(d) a management account

99. A company's annual trading and profit and loss account shows:

(a) the assets of the company and its liabilities
(b) payments received and expenditure incurred
(c) the current market value of the company's vehicles and fixed assets
(d) the value of its debtor and creditor accounts

100. From the following figures, which appear in the balance sheet of XY Haulage Limited, determine the amount of total capital employed.

	£		£
Share Capital	140,000	Property	110,000
Debentures	20,000	Motor vehicles	36,000
Creditors	24,000	Debtors	36,000
Bank overdraft	6,000	Cash reserves	8,000
	£190,000		£190,000

(a) £140,000
(b) £160,000
(c) £166,000
(d) £190,000

101. Which of the companies shown below achieves the highest rate of return on capital employed?

	Company A	Company B	Company C	Company D
	£	£	£	£
Issued Share Capital	100,000	200,000	300,000	400,000
Net Profit	20,000	30,000	40,000	50,000

(a) company A
(b) company B
(c) company C
(d) company D

102. What is the percentage rate of return on total capital employed for a firm which produces a balance sheet showing the following figures?

Issued Share Capital	£175,000
Bank overdraft	25,000
Gross Profit	40,000
Net Profit	25,000

(a) 12.5 per cent
(b) 15 per cent
(c) 20 per cent
(d) 25 per cent

103. The total capital employed in a business can be established by taking:

(a) its fixed assets plus its current assets
(b) its current liabilities plus its current assets
(c) its fixed assets minus its current assets
(d) its fixed and current assets minus its current liabilities

104. A business which is said to be under-capitalised suffers from:

(a) too few paid up shareholders
(b) a low value of fixed assets compared to current assets
(c) insufficient low interest loans
(d) too low a ratio of current assets to current liabilities

105. Which of the following figures must be available to enable return on capital employed to be calculated?

(a) net profit
(b) gross profit
(c) current assets
(d) current liabilities

106. The figure representing the total capital employed in a business is the total of its issued share capital and reserves, plus any:

(a) credit balance at the bank and cash in hand
(b) long-term loans
(c) unpaid debtors
(d) current assets

107. A company's fixed and current assets less the value of its current liabilities is a description of:

(a) its net worth
(b) its working capital
(c) its trading profit
(d) its total capital employed

108. A company's return on capital can be established from which of the following ratios?

(a) net profit divided by capital employed
(b) current assets divided by current liabilities
(c) total annual sales divided by total capital employed
(d) annual turnover divided by total sales

109. Which of the following accounting terms describes the working capital of a business?

(a) the value of plant, machinery and vehicles
(b) the ordinary share capital of the business
(c) petty cash in hand plus credit balances at the bank
(d) current assets less current liabilities

110. Which of the following operating expenses are debited against a firm's working capital?

(a) payment for diesel fuel
(b) capital invested in new workshop equipment
(c) the purchase of new and replacement vehicles
(d) the acquisition of a new office computer

111. Which of the following items would be described as a current liability?

(a) a bank overdraft
(b) the value of stocks held
(c) the amount of a firm's debtors
(d) the contents of a petty cash float

112. The working capital ratio of a business can be established by comparing:

- **(a) its creditors to debtors**
- **(b) its net profit to the total capital employed**
- **(c) its excess of current assets over current liabilities**
- **(d) its petty cash float to the bank overdraft**

113. What is a firm's working capital ratio if its current assets are £40,000 and its current liabilities are £20,000?

- **(a) 1:1**
- **(b) 1:2**
- **(c) 2:1**
- **(d) 5:1**

114. If a company's annual accounts show a profit, allowing for corporation tax, of £45,000 and the value of net assets as £180,000, its return on net assets will be:

- **(a) 2.5 per cent**
- **(b) 12. 5 per cent**
- **(c) 25 per cent**
- **(d) 45 per cent**

115. Which financial ratio can be calculated from a firm's trading and profit and loss account?

- **(a) total capital employed as a percentage of annual turnover**
- **(b) current ratio**
- **(c) gross profit as a percentage of annual turnover**
- **(d) liquidity ratio**

116. A firm with liquid assets of £315,000, a stock holding worth £220,000 and current liabilities of £150,000 has an acid test ratio of:

- **(a) 0.5:1**
- **(b) 1.2:1**
- **(c) 1.5:1**
- **(b) 2.1:1**

117. The usual formula for calculating current ratio is:

(a) liquid working capital divided by current liabilities
(b) current assets divided by current liabilities
(c) annual net profit divided by total capital employed
(d) bad debts divided by the value of current assets

118. Which of the following current ratios calculated from a company balance sheet would be considered the most favourable?

(a) 0.25:1
(b) 0.5:1
(c) 1:1
(d) 2:1

119. With current assets of £1,000,000 and current liabilities of £500,000 a firm has a current ratio of:

(a) 2:1
(b) 2.5:1
(c) 3:1
(d) 4:1

120. If a company's annual accounts show current assets of £75,600 and current liabilities of £36,000 its current ratio will be:

(a) 1:1
(b) 1:2
(c) 2:1
(d) 2.1:1

121. A firm's liquid assets divided by its current liabilities is a statement of:

(a) its liquidity ratio
(b) its current ratio
(c) its interest cover
(d) its debtor/creditor ratio

122. A firm with a liquidity ratio of 0.5:1 would:

(a) be in a healthy position
(b) have a high level of sales
(c) suffer from cash-flow problems

(d) be technically insolvent

123. A company with annual accounts showing liquid assets of £60,000 and current liabilities of £85,000 has a liquidity ratio of:

(a) 1:1
(b) 0.6:1
(c) 0.85:1
(d) 0.7:1

124. A creditor of a company is a person or firm:

(a) who owes the company money
(b) who grants credit to the company
(c) to whom the company grants credit
(d) to whom the company owes money

125. A creditor would appear in a firm's balance sheet as:

(a) a fixed asset
(b) a current asset
(c) part of its share capital
(d) a current liability

126. Money owed to a business by its customers is shown in its balance sheet under the heading:

(a) fixed assets
(b) creditors
(c) debtors
(d) unpaid loans

127. A firm's debtors are those:

(a) who owe it money for work/supplies invoiced
(b) to whom it owes money
(c) from whom it has obtained loans
(d) taking legal action against it for non-payment of debts

128. On default of payment of its debts, a firm's creditors may apply to a court for it to be compulsorily 'wound up'.

(a) True
(b) False

129. If a company has been voluntarily 'wound up', the liquidator is released from his duty:

(a) on authorisation from the Official Receiver
(b) on authorisation from the Registrar of Companies
(c) on application by the creditors to the Department of Trade and Industry
(d) by a resolution of both shareholders and creditors at the final creditor's meeting

A6 Capital and Cash Flow

130. Which of the following best describes the effects of 'cash flow' in business?

(a) cash received less debts owing to the business
(b) funds received and cash paid out by the business
(c) cash flowing out of the business to meet day-to-day commitments
(d) net profits made by the business

131. Which of the following financial measures would not assist in raising funds for a business?

(a) an issue of preference shares
(b) a rights issue of ordinary shares
(c) raising a debenture
(d) a shareholder selling his shares

132. Firms usually overcome their short-term cash-flow problems by:

(a) an issue of debenture stock
(b) an issue of redeemable preference shares
(c) arranging overdraft facilities with their bank
(d) offering increased trade discounts to customers

133. When a firm is experiencing cash-flow difficulties, one way of overcoming this is to:

(a) make an effort to increase sales

(b) give customers longer periods of credit
(c) factor its sales invoices
(d) increase productivity by overtime working

134. Which of the following financial policies would improve a firm's cash flow?

(a) paying creditors promptly
(b) paying all accounts on receipt of purchase invoice
(c) purchasing early while prices are stable
(d) reducing the periods of credit given to debtors

135. A haulier could improve his cash flow position by:

(a) obtaining extended credit from suppliers
(b) allowing debtors longer periods to pay their accounts
(c) paying creditors more promptly
(d) purchasing new vehicles

136. A 'cash budget' could be defined as:

(a) a record of cash received by a business
(b) a record of the cash expenditure of a business
(c) a plan for ensuring future sales
(d) a plan for future cash income and expenditure

137. A business which needs to assess its likely cash position six months ahead needs to prepare:

(a) a half-yearly profit and loss account
(b) a review of last year's trading performance
(c) a cash-flow forecast
(d) an updated balance sheet

138. In haulage, as in any other business, if possible, foreseeable purchases should:

(a) be planned for action when cash outflow is at a peak
(b) be planned for action when cash inflow is at a peak
(c) be planned for action when cash inflow is at a low level
(d) not be planned for the future but actioned as soon as required

139. A cash-flow statement would be prepared by a firm to indicate:

(a) the inflows of cash from its trading activities
(b) how its cash resources have been utilised over a given period
(c) its cash balances at the end of the period
(d) the sources and uses of funds over a given period

A7 Purchasing and Stock Control

140. Why is it important to keep file copies of purchase orders?

(a) to check against the invoice when the goods are received
(b) to avoid pilferage of stock
(c) to ensure suppliers do not make short deliveries
(d) for checking stock movements

141. Buying for stock can be justified for which of the following reasons?

(a) items will be on hand avoiding delays until supplies arrive
(b) capital tied up in stocks cannot be diverted to other uses
(c) surplus stock can be always sold off later
(d) obsolete stock can be 'written-off' for tax purposes

142. Which of the following stocks would be classed as obsolete?

(a) stock for which demand is slow and irregular
(b) stock which is in high seasonal demand
(c) stock purchased in readiness for changing demand
(d) parts for equipment replaced by new and updated versions

143. Effective stock control in a heavy vehicle workshop will:

(a) result in accumulation of excessive stocks

(b) reduce the amount of capital reserves tied up in stock
(c) jeopardise the company's cash-flow position
(d) reduce the financial resources available for more pressing purposes

144. When carrying out a physical check of fuel stocks, the amount on hand should be:

(a) opening stock – deliveries from the supplier + issues to vehicles
(b) opening stock + deliveries from the supplier – issues to vehicles
(c) opening stock + issues to vehicles + deliveries from the supplier
(d) deliveries from the supplier – issues to vehicles + opening stock

145. On checking its fuel storage tank a haulage firm found its fuel stock was valued at £1,628. During the accounting period, fuel amounting to £2,785 had been delivered and a check on the previous balance showed an amount carried forward of £843. What was the value of fuel used during the period?

(a) £1,000
(b) £1,628
(c) £2,000
(d) £2,461

146. A firm's fuel storage tank held 2,603 litres at the start of a period and 27,400 litres of new stock was received. If 26,503 litres were issued how much fuel should now be in the tank?

(a) 503 litres
(b) 2,603 litres
(c) 3,500 litres
(d) 7,400 litres

147. If a person purchased 1,000 items at £20 each and sold 900 of them at £25 each, his gross profit from the sales is:

(a) £4,500
(b) £5,000
(c) £18,000
(d) £22,500

A8 Commercial Conduct of Business and Banking

148. In commercial transactions which of the following would constitute an order?

(a) a price list of charges for business services
(b) a request from a supplier for payment of money owed
(c) a form detailing goods consigned for delivery by public carrier
(d) a request by a customer to be supplied with goods or services.

149. For which of the following purposes is an advice note used ?

(a) to advise customers that goods are about to be delivered
(b) to advise customers that goods ordered are out of stock
(c) to advise a transport department to make a delivery
(d) to advise customers that quoted prices are subject to change

150. Which of the following documents should be used regularly by a haulier?

(a) a consignment note
(b) a bill of lading
(c) a cover note
(d) a debit note

151. The document carried on a vehicle showing delivery addresses, the number of consignments to be delivered and with a space for the consignee to sign as having received the goods is known as:

(a) an invoice

(b) a waybill
(c) a consignment note
(d) a bill of lading

152. A haulier considering the repair of a badly damaged vehicle asks a garage about the likely cost. The garage will initially provide:

(a) an invoice for the work
(b) an order for the job
(c) a statement of the cost
(d) an estimate of labour time and materials

153. A firm requested to specify the cost of its services and state whether credit terms are available does so by means of:

(a) an invoice
(b) a statement
(c) a credit note
(d) a quotation

154. A quotation is a formal notification, usually in writing:

(a) from a supplier to a customer stating the amount owed for work done
(b) from a customer requesting the supply of goods or services
(c) from a supplier reminding a customer how his account stands
(d) to a customer giving a specific price for a particular job

155. Due to a clerical error in preparing an invoice a haulier undercharges a customer for work done. The haulier would correct this by:
(a) sending the customer a statement of account
(b) sending the customer a debit note
(c) making necessary alterations on the invoice
(d) issuing the customer with a credit note

156. When might a purchaser request a credit note in his favour?

(a) if damaged goods have been returned to him
(b) if he returns damaged goods to the supplier
(c) to ensure prompt payment of his account
(d) to ensure the vendor pays his account promptly

157. The document issued in business to correct an overcharge on an invoice is called:

(a) a tender
(b) a debit note
(c) a statement
(d) a credit note

158. In which of the following circumstances might a credit note be issued?

(a) when charges for goods supplied are omitted from an invoice
(b) when a customer is due for a refund
(c) when goods were undercharged on the invoice
(d) to show a customer how his account stands

159. A road haulier would send customers a request for payment for work done by means of:

(a) a debit note
(b) a proof of delivery note
(c) an invoice
(d) a statement

160. A statement of account is a commercial document:

(a) used for invoicing export consignments
(b) reminding a customer how his account stands with the supplier
(c) notifying customers of the price for carrying out a job
(d) sent by a purchaser confirming acceptance of the price charged

161. Which of the following is the best example of the correct use of the term 'account rendered'?

(a) for goods and services invoiced and paid for
(b) for goods and services paid for but not yet supplied

(c) for goods and services invoiced for payment
(d) for goods and services for which the account has been returned as incorrect

162. Statements of account are sent to customers to:

(a) show their total indebtedness to the supplier at a particular date
(b) show the credit limit allowed by the supplier
(c) show the amounts charged by the supplier for goods or services
(d) charge for additional operating expenses not known at the time the original invoice was raised

163. Which of the following details do not normally appear on a statement of account?

(a) adjustments for debit and credit notes issued
(b) discounts available to the customer for prompt payment
(c) totals of the invoices issued during the period
(d) descriptions of the goods or services supplied

164. A customer denies receiving certain goods although proof exists that they were delivered, so he is sent a copy of the document he signed when receiving them. A copy of which commercial document would be sent?

(a) the consignment note relating to the delivery
(b) the advice note notifying delivery
(c) the invoice for the job
(d) the order form requesting delivery

165. Which of the following bank accounts would a haulier open to lodge day-to-day receipts and issue cheques to pay business expenses?

(a) a savings account
(b) a current account
(c) a deposit account
(d) a budget account

166. To ensure a cheque can be paid only into a named bank account it should be:

(a) left open
(b) clearly crossed with two heavy lines
(c) crossed with the words '& Co' between the crossing lines
(d) crossed with the words 'a/c payee' between the crossing lines

167. A bank account which allows use of the cheque system is called:

(a) a high-interest deposit account
(b) a Giro account
(c) a current account
(d) a deposit account

168. The main advantage to the recipient of a 'banker's draft' is that:

(a) it can be converted into cash
(b) the bank on which it is drawn must honour it when it is presented
(c) it does not have to be cashed through a bank account
(d) interest will be paid on it if it is not cashed within six months

169. In a cheque transaction, which of the following is the payee of the cheque?

(a) the bank on which the cheque is drawn
(b) the individual on whose account the cheque is drawn
(c) the person or firm to whom payment is to be made
(d) the individual who pays in the cheque to the bank

170. Cheques are normally honoured by the banks only if they are presented within a certain period of the date shown. This period is:

(a) 3 months
(b) 6 months
(c) 9 months
(d) 12 months

171. A haulage driver who has no bank account asks his employer to pay his wages by a cheque that he can

readily change into cash. The employer would need to give him:

(a) a crossed cheque
(b) a cheque crossed ' & Co'
(c) a cheque crossed 'a/c payee'
(d) an open cheque

172. A returned cheque marked 'Refer to drawer' means there are insufficient funds in the account of the drawer to cover the amount shown.

(a) True
(b) False

173. With the direct debit system of regular payments from a bank account it is a disadvantage to the debtor because:

(a) his creditors have access to details of his bank account
(b) payments do not take account of monthly fluctuations
(c) he does not always know the amount debited to his account
(d) he cannot delay payment of an account

174. Credit transfer is a means of paying for goods or services:

(a) by computerised invoicing
(b) using Access, Visa or a similar type of credit card
(c) direct into the creditor's bank account
(d) using a bankers' cheque card

175. When a firm decides to pay suppliers' accounts direct to its bank rather than by issuing cheques, it would set-up a system known as:

(a) deferred credit
(b) direct debit
(c) standing order
(d) credit transfer

176. Which of the following statements describes payment of a 'bearer' cheque at a bank?

(a) only the named payee may cash it but it must be endorsed
(b) the person presenting it can only have it paid into an account
(c) only the named payee may cash it
(d) anyone presenting it to the bank on which it is drawn may receive cash against it

A9 General Insurance

177. Besides third party motor insurance, against which of the following additional risks must a haulier legally have insurance cover?

(a) passenger liability
(b) accidental damage to his own vehicles
(c) loss by fire
(d) theft from his own vehicles

178. A road haulage company is required by law to have which of the following types of insurance cover?

(a) goods in transit
(b) fire
(c) employers' liability
(d) fidelity guarantee

179. A driver's mate, carried on a haulage vehicle in the course of his work, would be covered for personal injury under the terms of his firm's:

(a) consequential loss insurance
(b) third party insurance
(c) fidelity guarantee insurance
(d) employers' liability insurance

180. Compulsory employers' liability insurance is intended to cover claims:

(a) by customers injured by using defective products
(b) by employees alleging unfair dismissal
(c) by employees injured at work
(d) for loss of production due to industrial action

181. A road haulier wishing to cover against loss of trade in the event of a fire at his premises would take out which of the following types of policy?

(a) consequential loss
(b) loss by fire
(c) public liability
(d) employers' liability

182. A haulier wishing to insure against liabilities for death or injury to a third party, as a result of the defective loading of one of his vehicles, would take out a policy covering:

(a) consequential loss
(b) public liability
(c) third party risks
(d) employers' liability

183. A haulage vehicle loaded with empty drums is being driven on a road when one of the drums falls off causing damage to a following vehicle. What type of insurance would cover the driver's employer for the damage to the following vehicle?

(a) goods in transit
(b) employers' liability
(c) fidelity guarantee
(d) public liability

184. Loss of company property due to an employee's fraudulent actions is normally covered by which of the following insurances?

(a) employers' liability
(b) fidelity guarantee
(c) consequential loss
(d) third party risks

185. A person sustains injury while visiting a haulier's premises. What type of insurance would cover the haulier against the claim for damages?

(a) consequential loss
(b) fidelity guarantee
(c) employers' liability
(d) public liability

186. Which of the following types of insurance covers against loss of goods carried on a vehicle?

(a) theft
(b) goods in transit
(c) employers' liability
(d) motor vehicle

187. Which of the following types of insurance would provide cover against loss of property as a result of thieves gaining entry to premises?

(a) public liability cover
(b) endowment insurance
(c) all risks insurance
(d) third party motor cover

188. The 'excess clause' in a goods in transit insurance policy means that:

(a) goods held for an excessive period are no longer covered
(b) the operator is responsible for paying the first part of each claim
(c) goods carried for an excessive distance are not covered
(d) claims in excess of a certain value are not covered

189. An 'immobiliser' clause in a goods in transit insurance policy means that the vehicle:

(a) must not be left unattended on a road at night
(b) must be fitted with an approved anti-theft device
(c) must only be parked in approved parks overnight.
(d) is not to carry goods during the hours of darkness

190. A restrictive 'night risk' clause contained in a goods in transit policy means that:

(a) goods must be transported only during the hours of daylight
(b) goods will automatically be covered against the additional risks of night transport
(c) vehicles must not be left unattended at night unless fitted with approved anti-theft devices
(d) goods of very high value must not be transported at night unless special insurance cover is obtained

A10 Structure of Law and Liability

191. Which of the following is an example of statute law?

- (a) The Road Vehicles (Construction and Use) Regulations 1986
- (b) Motor Vehicles (Authorisation of Special Types) General Order 1979
- (c) The Road Traffic Act 1988
- (d) Road Vehicles (Registration and Licensing) Regulations 1971

192. Law made by Parliament is called:

- (a) common law
- (b) statute law
- (c) canon law
- (d) case law

193. Which of the following is an example of subordinate legislation?

- (a) a decision made in a court of law
- (b) The Transport Act 1968
- (c) The Road Vehicles Lighting Regulations 1984
- (d) The Health and Safety at Work etc. Act 1975

194. To be legally enforceable all contracts must comprise:

- (a) an offer only
- (b) an offer and an acceptance
- (c) an offer, acceptance and consideration
- (d) an offer, acceptance, consideration and confirmation in writing

195. If a court upholds a breach of contract action this usually results in:

- (a) the defendant being fined
- (b) the plaintiff receiving an award of damages
- (c) the defendant being given a term of imprisonment
- (d) a ban on both plaintiff and defendant entering into further contracts with each other

196. Which of the following is not necessary for a contract to be legally valid?

(a) the offer
(b) a consideration
(c) the acceptance
(d) confirmation in writing

197. **In law a contract legally exists when:**

(a) one party has done all that it contracted to do
(b) it is confirmed in writing
(c) both parties have done what they contracted to do
(d) an offer has been accepted

198. **A contract made verbally between parties:**

(a) has no validity in law
(b) is legally enforceable provided it is confirmed in writing
(c) would be legally binding in an emergency situation
(d) is legally binding on the parties concerned

199. **In contract terms, an offer is deemed to be accepted when:**

(a) both parties fulfil what they have each contracted to do
(b) the party accepting an offer has fulfilled what he contracted to do
(c) the person to whom an offer is made accepts the contract terms
(d) the person to whom an offer is made communicates his acceptance to the person making the offer

200. **Under the law of contract, an offer may be withdrawn at:**

(a) any time
(b) any time before it is accepted
(c) any time after it is accepted
(d) any time providing the withdrawal is made in writing

201. **When negotiating contracts, if an offer is made but subject to specified conditions, the offeree must be made aware of those conditions:**

(a) as soon as possible
(b) at or before the time the contract is made
(c) no later than 24 hours after the contract is made
(d) no later than 7 days after the contract is made

202. In contract law, the term 'consideration' is taken to mean that:

(a) each party must derive a benefit from the contract
(b) all the parties involved must behave fairly towards each other
(c) the parties must think carefully before they make the contract
(d) each party must ensure they interpret the contract terms identically

203. A claim for damages as a result of alleged negligence on the part of a haulier can be successful only if:

(a) the haulier failed to fulfil a statutory obligation
(b) the negligence arose from a criminal action
(c) the haulier had a legally binding contract with the plaintiff
(d) the plaintiff can show that he has suffered a loss

204. In business relationships, which of the following is not legally considered to be an agent?

(a) a factor
(b) a broker
(c) a principal
(d) an auctioneer

205. An authorised agent acting on commission for a haulier arranged for collection and delivery of a customer's goods, but due to over-booking the customer's schedules could not be met and he claims substantial losses as a result of this. How do the parties legally stand?

(a) the customer can sue the agent for his losses
(b) the customer can sue the haulier alone for his losses in full
(c) the customer can sue both the haulier and the agent jointly for any loss

(d) there can be no claim as this is one of the hazards of using hauliers

206. When a contract is made by an agent on behalf of his principal, this contract is binding on:

(a) both the agent and the third party
(b) both the principal and his agent
(c) both the principal and the third party
(d) the principal, the agent and the third party

207. If an authorised agent makes secret profits from his business dealings with customers on behalf of his principal:

(a) the principal can sue his agent for an amount equal to those profits
(b) the agent can keep the profits whether or not the principal suffered any loss
(c) the profits must be returned to the customers from whom they were obtained
(d) the agent may keep the profits so long as the principal suffered no loss

208. A haulier who accepts haulage work subject to the terms set out in his conditions of carriage restricts his legal liability to that of:

(a) a common carrier
(b) a private carrier
(c) a limited liability carrier
(d) a public liability carrier

209. Which of the following organisations publishes standard road haulage industry conditions of carriage?

(a) the Road Haulage Association
(b) the Freight Transport Association
(c) the Office of Fair Trading
(d) the Department of Trade and Industry

210. A road haulier can legally restrict liability to his customers by:

(a) only employing reliable staff under strict conditions of employment
(b) only undertaking haulage work in accordance with his published Conditions of Carriage
(c) ensuring that an appropriate disclaimer is included in his company's Articles of Association.
(d) sending to customers a copy of his Memorandum of Association.

211. A haulage company's conditions of carriage are legally binding provided that:

(a) copies are sent to the customer after the delivery has been made
(b) they are printed on the back of collection notes
(c) the driver carries a copy in his cab
(d) they are drawn to the attention of customers before contracts for haulage are made

212. Which of the following factors would not normally be found in standard conditions of carriage?

(a) specification of the make of vehicles to be used
(b) specified loading and unloading conditions
(c) detailed requirements regarding the labelling of goods
(d) limits on financial liability for loss of or damage to goods

213. Which of the following liability conditions apply to contracts of carriage with both private and common carriers?

(a) carriers are liable for loss resulting only from their own negligence
(b) carriers cannot limit their liability except against Acts of God or other 'excepted perils'
(c) documentary evidence of a contract is not required
(d) these conditions do not apply to either private or common carriers

214. Rights of a carrier to hold goods until he has been paid for his services is legally known by the term:

(a) a bond
(b) a lien
(c) a warranty
(d) a power of detention

215. A private carrier would be held liable for loss of or damage to a customer's goods if it could be proven that it was due to negligence on the part of the:

(a) consignor's staff who inadequately packed the goods
(b) consignor's staff who mis-labelled the goods
(c) consignee
(d) carrier's employees

216. The meaning of the legal term 'particular lien' in relation to road haulage is that:

(a) the carrier must specify a particular date by which carriage charges are due for payment
(b) the carrier may detain goods carried until carriage charges for moving those particular goods are paid
(c) the carrier may detain the goods carried for a particular period of time until carriage charges are paid
(d) the carrier may detain any of the owner's goods until all outstanding carriage charges are paid

217. Where a haulier sub-contracts work to a third party haulier and this results in loss of a customer's goods:

(a) he is liable to the customer for the full amount of the claim
(b) he would only be liable to meet the customer's claim if the sub-contractor fails to do so
(c) he could not be held liable to the customer in these circumstances
(d) he cannot be held liable if the customer was informed in advance of the name of the sub-contractor who was to transport the goods

218. If a haulier's fleet is fully committed but he still accepts additional work:

(a) a contract exists therefore the work can only be sub-contracted at the original price.
(b) a contract exists therefore the haulier must shelve his present commitments to carry out the work
(c) the haulier may sub-contract the work but must inform the sub-contracted haulier the price charged to the customer
(d) the haulier may sub-contract the work without advising the sub-contracted haulier the price charged to the customer

219. Vicarious liability means that an employer is responsible for the negligent actions of his employee while the employee is acting within the scope of his authority?

(a) True
(b) False

220. A petrol tanker driver who causes an explosion at a petrol filling station through lighting a cigarette would be considered to be guilty of:

(a) breach of his contract of employment
(b) an act of arson
(c) criminal negligence
(d) failing to take due care

221. A plaintiff's claim for damages as a result of a haulier's negligence could only be successful if:

(a) the plaintiff has suffered loss or injury
(b) it could be proved that the haulier had broken the law
(c) the haulier had entered into a valid legal contract with the plaintiff
(d) the haulier has committed a criminal offence

222. Where a person suffers injury as the result of the action of an employee in the course of his duties:

(a) he may sue the employee only
(b) the may sue the employee's employer only
(c) he may sue both employee and employer

(d) as this was an accident that happened at work he cannot sue anyone

223. An occupier of premises owes a common duty of care towards both visitors and employees under the:

(a) Health and Safety at Work etc. Act 1974
(b) Landowners' Act 1878
(c) Employment Protection (Consolidation) Act 1978
(d) Occupiers Liability Act 1957 (as amended)

224. Occupiers of premises:

(a) must take reasonable care to safeguard trespassers on their premises
(b) can set man-traps and use loose guard dogs to deter trespassers
(c) cannot sue a trespasser even if he causes damage to the premises
(d) have no legal duty of care towards trespassers

225. A person who is injured when visiting company-owned premises:

(a) would be able to seek damages if negligence could be proved against the company
(b) would be able to seek damages only if he was injured as a result of the work activity of an employee at the premises
(c) would not be able to claim damages if, at the time he sustained injury, he was trespassing on the premises
(d) would not be able to claim damages against the company under any circumstances

226. A haulier permits his driver to take a vehicle home each night and at weekends, where it remains parked in the street outside his house. Local residents complain that it blocks the street and causes them a private nuisance by depriving them of light. Who in law is liable for the nuisance?

(a) the driver alone
(b) the operator alone

(c) both driver and operator
(d) there is no liability by either party as the vehicle is parked on a public road

227. Which of the following constitutes a public nuisance?

(a) causing disturbance with excessive noise late at night
(b) causing pollution by dumping waste oil on private land
(c) obstructing the gateway to private land with a vehicle.
(d) blocking a busy street with a lorry which has shed part of its load

228. A haulier who allows smoke from a bonfire on his premises to spoil a neighbour's enjoyment of his garden would constitute what form of tort?

(a) public nuisance
(b) private nuisance
(c) trespass
(d) negligence

229. A haulier whose premises adjoin a row of private houses is sued by one of the householders who claims that the activities of the firm substantially interfere with enjoyment of the land which he occupies. If a court upheld the householder's claim, the haulier would be found to have committed the tort of:

(a) trespass
(b) public nuisance
(c) private nuisance
(d) negligence

230. When goods are sold on a credit sale arrangement they become the legal property of the purchaser:

(a) after six months from the date of sale
(b) when half of the total number of instalments have been paid
(c) when all instalments have been paid
(d) when a deposit or the first instalment has been paid

A11 Business and Company Law

231. A partnership would automatically be dissolved if:

- (a) any one of the partners died or became bankrupt
- (b) any one of the partners said he was resigning
- (c) any one of the partners was unable or unwilling to continue working
- (d) one partner sacked the other partners

232. If a person intends trading as a haulage contractor under a name other than his own he must:

- (a) notify the Department of Transport
- (b) register the name with the Department of Trade and Industry
- (c) display his name and the trading name at his place of business
- (d) register the trading name with the Registrar of Business Names

233. Where two or more persons enter into a partnership arrangement:

- (a) each individual partner will be responsible only for his or her own personal actions
- (b) partners may legally negotiate individual business contracts with the partnership
- (c) the action of each individual partner is legally binding on the other partners
- (d) individual partners are not legally empowered to act for the partnership without the specific authority of the other partners

234. A partner in a haulage firm is:

- (a) personally liable for all debts incurred by the partnership
- (b) not personally liable for any business debt incurred by the partnership
- (c) liable only for a proportion of the partnership debts in accordance with his share of the partnership
- (d) not liable for business debts incurred by his partners without his knowledge

235. **Any business, apart from a public limited company, which trades as a registered company must, under the provisions of the Companies Act, have a name ending with the letters or word:**

(a) incorporated
(b) company
(c) limited
(d) plc

236. **When a private limited company wishes to increase its share capital under the provisions of the Companies Act it may:**

(a) not advertise for the public to subscribe for shares
(b) advertise the availability of shares to the public
(c) publicly offer to exchange new shares for capital investment
(d) not offer any share holding beyond the existing list of shareholders

237. **A private limited company must have at least:**

(a) one shareholder
(b) two shareholders
(c) four shareholders
(d) seven shareholders

238. **The term 'share capital' is used in company law to mean:**

(a) the share of business profits paid to shareholders in dividends
(b) the capital invested in a company by its shareholders
(c) the method for allocating dividends among shareholders
(d) the total capital employed as shown in the balance sheet

239. **To enable a newly registered limited liability company to operate legally, it must have the minimum number of shareholders and they must sign:**

(a) the Declaration of Incorporation

(b) the Articles of Association
(c) the Memorandum of Association
(d) a Certificate of Incorporation.

240. When a limited liability company is to be prosecuted for an offence, this is addressed to and answerable by:

(a) the company secretary
(b) the chairman
(c) the managing director
(d) the board of directors collectively

241. The objects of a company are set out in its:

(a) Certificate of Incorporation
(b) Annual Report
(c) Articles of Association
(d) Memorandum of Association

242. A recently formed limited liability company is required to hold its first Annual General Meeting (AGM) of members within:

(a) 6 months
(b) 12 months
(c) 18 months
(d) 24 months

243. A written notice of the annual general meeting for a company must be sent to all members at least:

(a) 7 days in advance
(b) 14 days in advance
(c) 21 days in advance
(d) 28 days in advance

244. Which type of general meeting could be called by a quorum of shareholders in a limited liability company to discuss an important business matter?

(a) a board meeting
(b) an annual general meeting
(c) a directors' meeting
(d) an extraordinary general meeting

245. What minimum number of shareholder members of a public limited company must sign the company's Memorandum of Association?

(a) 2
(b) 3
(c) 7
(d) 12

246. The legal statement of the purposes for which a private limited liability company is established and of the liability of its members is called:

(a) the Register
(b) a Certificate of Incorporation
(c) the Memorandum of Association
(d) the Articles of Association

247. The Articles of Association of a limited liability company is a document:

(a) containing a list of each shareholder's name
(b) sent by way of a prospectus to potential shareholders in the company
(c) setting out the objects for which the company was established
(d) setting out the rules governing the internal working of the company

248. A public limited company must have a name ending with the letters or words:

(a) company limited
(b) limited
(c) plc
(d) incorporated

249. A public limited company is required to have at least:

(a) 2 members
(b) 7 members
(c) 10 members
(d) 100 members

250. A public limited company must have a minimum authorised share capital of at least:

(a) £1,000
(b) £50,000

(c) £500,000
(d) £1,000,000

251. Under the provisions of the Companies Act, company directors are required to have specific regard to the interests of:

(a) the shareholders only
(b) both employees and shareholders
(c) employees only
(d) employees, shareholders and suppliers

252. The legal requirement for company directors' reports to contain a statement about employee involvement applies in firms which have:

(a) not more than 25 employees
(b) not more than 250 employees
(c) more than 25 employees
(d) more than 250 employees

253. Which of the following classes of shareholder always has voting rights in a company?

(a) ordinary shareholders
(b) preference shareholders
(c) debenture holders
(d) shareholder directors

254. The statutory rights of shareholders in a limited liability company are to be found in the company's:

(a) Annual Report
(b) Certificate of Incorporation
(c) Memorandum of Association
(d) Articles of Association

255. If a creditor obtains a company winding-up order from a court the resulting action on the part of the company would be called:

(a) a statutory meeting of creditors
(b) voluntary liquidation
(c) compulsory liquidation
(d) declaration of bankruptcy

A12 Industrial Relations

256. The Advisory Conciliation and Arbitration Service (ACAS) is:

(a) an agency of the TUC
(b) a department within the Department of Employment
(c) a statutory institution
(d) a department of the CBI

257. The role of the Advisory, Conciliation and Arbitration Service is to:

(a) represent trade unions in dispute with company managements
(b) represent employees in dispute with employers
(c) resolve issues between employers and employees in dispute
(d) offer advice to employees, employers, trade associations and trade unions

258. If ACAS is not successful in settling a dispute, the next legal step which can be taken is:

(a) to refer the matter to the CAC
(b) to refer the matter to the Licensing Authority
(c) to refer the matter to the DTi
(d) no further action

259. The Trade Union and Labour Relations Act 1974, as amended, gives employees which of the following rights regarding union membership?

(a) no right to belong to a trade union
(b) no rights either to belong or not to belong to a trade union
(c) a right to belong or not to belong to a trade union
(d) a right to belong but no right not to belong to a trade union

260. Under the Employment Act 1980, in order to establish an approved union membership agreement, the agreement must be ratified in secret ballot by:

(a) all of those who voted
(b) 80 per cent of those who voted
(c) all of those entitled to vote
(d) 80 per cent of those entitled to vote

261. The Central Arbitration Committee was set up to deal with complaints about:

(a) appeals against unfair dismissal
(b) failure by an employer to recognise an independent trade union
(c) failure by an employer to disclose information
(d) unfair contract of employment terms

262. Collective bargaining as a means of establishing workers' pay is encouraged under which of the following Acts?

(a) Industrial Relations Act 1971
(b) Employment Protection Act 1975
(c) Trade Union and Labour Relations Act 1974
(d) Contracts of Employment Act 1972

263. For the purposes of employment law, a full-time worker is one who works more than:

(a) 10 hours per week
(b) 12 hours per week
(c) 16 hours per week
(d) 24 hours per week

264. Picketing in furtherance of a trade dispute is legally permitted so long as:

(a) it peacefully attempts to persuade employees to work or not work
(b) it prevents employees only from entering the work premises
(c) it takes place only on the employer's premises
(d) the police have given specific permission for it to take place

265. Secondary action taken in furtherance of a trade dispute is action taken:

(a) in sympathy with a strike
(b) to disrupt supplies between the employer in dispute and his suppliers
(c) against customers of the employer with whom the dispute exists
(d) against employees who are not involved in the dispute

266. An employee is legally entitled to a minimum of one week's notice of dismissal after he has completed:

(a) 4 weeks' service
(b) 12 weeks' service
(c) 13 weeks' service
(d) 26 weeks' service

267. An employee who wishes to terminate his employment must give his employer at least one week's notice:

(a) after he has been employed for one week
(b) after he has been employed for two weeks or more
(c) after he has been employed for one month or more
(d) irrespective of how long he has been employed

268. An employee with 5 years and 11 months of continuous service is entitled to receive the following period of notice from his employer on termination of employment:

(a) 3 weeks
(b) 4 weeks
(c) 5 weeks
(d) 6 weeks

269. The onus is on an employer to show that dismissal of an employee was reasonable in all the circumstances.

(a) True
(b) False

270. Firms established for less than 2 years employing fewer than a certain number of people are exempted from the unfair dismissal provisions. The number is:

(a) 5

(b) 12
(c) 18
(d) 20

271. The statutory time limit within which a dismissed employee can make an unfair dismissal claim to an industrial tribunal is:

(a) 6 months
(b) 3 months
(c) 2 months
(d) 1 month

272. A claim to an industrial tribunal for unfair dismissal cannot be made unless the employee has completed a minimum of:

(a) 13 weeks' service
(b) 26 weeks' service
(c) 52 weeks' service
(d) 104 weeks' service

273. An employee who is dismissed after completing at least 4 weeks continuous service with an employer:

(a) is not entitled to a written statement of the reasons for dismissal
(b) is not entitled to a written statement if dismissed for misconduct
(c) must be given a written statement of the reasons on request
(d) must always be given a written statement of the reasons for dismissal

274. In a claim before an industrial tribunal for unfair dismissal, the burden of proof as to whether the dismissal was fair or unfair rests with:

(a) ACAS
(b) the employer only
(c) both the employer and employee
(d) the dismissed person

275. An employee who has been dismissed is entitled to a written reason for dismissal:

(a) irrespective of the reasons for dismissal
(b) under no circumstances
(c) only if the employee specifically requests it
(d) only if the employee has at least 2 years' service with the employer

276. Where a person claims dismissal was due to trade union membership and activities, the industrial tribunal accepting the complaint would:

(a) order reinstatement or re-engagement only
(b) order reinstatement or re-engagement and make a 'special' award
(c) make a basic award only
(d) make a compensatory award only

277. Which of the following employees may claim unfair dismissal?

(a) a man aged 25 years with 3 years' continuous employment
(b) a woman aged 62 with 11 years' continuous employment
(c) a part-time employee
(d) an employee who normally works overseas

278. Which of the following is an unfair reason for dismissal?

(a) refusing to join a trade union when there is a closed shop
(b) being a member of a trade union
(c) the lack of suitable qualifications
(d) where a particular job becomes redundant

279. When an employer plans to make between 10 and 99 employees redundant over a period of 30 days, the Employment Secretary must be notified at least:

(a) 10 days in advance
(b) 30 days in advance
(c) 60 days in advance
(d) 90 days in advance

280. Which of the following persons made redundant would be eligible to claim statutory redundancy payment?

(a) an employee aged 20 and employed continuously for 3 years
(b) an employee aged 32 and employed continuously for 18 months
(c) a man aged 64 and employed continuously for 5 years
(d) a woman aged 60 and employed continuously for 25 years

281. Which of the following persons would not be entitled to a statutory redundancy payment?

(a) a man aged 28 with 18 months' service with his employer
(b) a woman aged 20 with 2 years' service with her employer
(c) a man aged 65 with 3 years' service with his employer
(d) a woman aged 60 with 10 years' service with her employer

282. Which of the following classes of employee is covered by legal provisions relating to redundancy payments?

(a) a part-timer with 2 years' service working 12 hours weekly
(b) a female senior executive aged 61 years
(c) a full-timer with 3 years' continuous service
(d) a person who is self-employed

283. A redundant employee who refuses a reasonable offer of suitable alternative employment with a subsidiary of his present employer would not be entitled to a redundancy payment.

(a) True
(b) False

284. Redundancy payments are calculated on the basis of:

(a) length of service, and sex
(b) age, length of service and weekly earnings
(c) weekly earnings only
(d) sex, age and service

285. In calculating a statutory redundancy payment, qualifying service over the age of 22 years and under 41 years counts for payment at a rate of:

(a) half of one week's pay for each complete year of service
(b) one weeks' pay for each complete year of service
(c) 1.5 weeks' pay for each complete year of service
(d) two weeks' pay for each complete year of service

286. A person employed by a firm for 1 year and 11 months who is made redundant would be entitled to a statutory minimum period of notice of:

(a) 1 week
(b) 2 weeks
(c) 3 weeks
(d) 4 weeks

287. When calculating an employee's continuous service for the purposes of determining a redundancy payment, any time he was on strike is:

(a) included only if the total service exceeds 2 years
(b) included in the total period of continuous service
(c) included providing the strike was recognised by a trade union
(d) not included in the total period of continuous service

288. The maximum period of continuous service with an employer that can be taken into account when calculating redundancy pay is:

(a) 5 years
(b) 10 years
(c) 15 years
(d) 20 years

289. An employer intending to create 10 or more redundancies within a 30 day period must notify the Employment Secretary and a recognised trade union in advance within a period of:

(a) 30 days

(b) 60 days
(c) 90 days
(d) 100 days

290. Employers must allow a trade union to conduct secret ballots on union matters on their premises if they have more than:

(a) 10 employees
(b) 20 employees
(c) 100 employees
(d) 200 employees

291. If an employer refuses to disclose information to a union under the terms of employment legislation when requested to do so, the union can make a complaint to:

(a) the Road Haulage Association
(b) ACAS
(c) the CAC
(d) the Road Transport Industry Training Board

292. What information must legally be disclosed to a recognised trade union within a firm under current employment legislation?

(a) all information requested
(b) details of the firm's future investment plans
(c) personal details of employees' ages and rates of pay
(d) information necessary for use in collective pay bargaining

293. What information need an employer not disclose to a trade union under consultative procedures for dealing with redundancies?

(a) the method used for selecting employees for redundancy
(b) the reasons for creating the redundancies
(c) the total number of persons employed at the establishment
(d) amounts to be paid in redundancy payments

294. Which of the following persons would be entitled under employment legislation to time off work with pay to carry out particular duties?

(a) a shop steward engaging in union business
(b) a union member wishing to attend a union meeting
(c) a person called up for jury service
(d) a Justice of the Peace to carry out his public duties

295. An employee who is an official of his local trade union branch can claim time off work for training in connection with those duties amounting to:

(a) up to 1 hour each day
(b) up to 3 days per week
(c) 4 days per week
(d) any amount of time that is reasonably necessary

296. Under employment legislation an official of an independent trade union is entitled to time off work with pay for the purposes of:

(a) attending local council meetings in his role as a local councillor
(b) attending official trade union duties and training
(c) undertaking his duties as a Justice of the Peace
(d) attending to official trade union duties only

297. An employee who is on the committee of a local educational establishment and has to attend occasional meetings during normal working hours:

(a) may have a reasonable amount of unpaid time off to attend meetings
(b) may have a reasonable amount of time off with pay to attend such meetings
(c) need not be given any time off to attend the meetings
(d) is only entitled to time off to attend meetings if he works extra time to compensate the employer for his absence

298. Which of the following benefits is not within the scope of wage council orders?

(a) employees' remuneration
(b) workers' holiday entitlements
(c) company manning levels
(d) conditions of employment

299. A contract of employment between an employer and employee exists:

(a) only if the offer of employment and acceptance are in writing
(b) when the employee has received a written statement of the terms and conditions of employment
(c) when the employer makes an offer of employment which is accepted by the employee
(d) once the employee has worked continuously for a period of 4 weeks

300. Which of the following terms should be included in a contract of employment?

(a) the employee's national insurance number
(b) the periods of notice required on termination of the employment
(c) the employee's educational and job qualifications
(d) details of the employee's interests and hobbies

301. An employer has a statutory duty to give a new employee a written statement of the main terms and conditions of his employment:

(a) prior to commencing the employment
(b) immediately on commencing the employment
(c) within 4 weeks of commencing the employment
(d) within 13 weeks of commencing the employment

302. If an employee's terms of employment are changed, he must be notified within what statutory period of time?

(a) 3 weeks
(b) 1 month
(c) 13 weeks
(d) 3 months

303. If an employee is suspended from work for medical reasons, he may be entitled to full pay for:

(a) at least 4 weeks
(b) 13 weeks
(c) 26 weeks
(d) 1 year

304. Female employees wishing to return to work after confinement must advise their employers of this fact in writing and give:

(a) 7 days' notice
(b) 14 days' notice
(c) 21 days' notice
(d) 28 days' notice

305. A female employee who is pregnant is:

(a) entitled to receive a reasonable amount of time off without pay to receive ante-natal care
(b) entitled to receive a reasonable amount of time off with pay to receive ante-natal care
(c) entitled to receive a reasonable amount of time off to receive ante-natal care but must make up this time later
(d) not entitled to any time off for ante-natal care

306. A woman who is claiming maternity leave normally has a right to return to work up to:

(a) 28 weeks after her confinement
(b) 49 weeks after her confinement
(c) 52 weeks after her confinement
(d) 58 weeks after her confinement

307. The Industrial Training Act deals with:

(a) building industrial estates to provide employment
(b) training employees engaged in industry
(c) the provision of investment capital for industry
(d) formulating industrial relations policies

308. What official body is responsible for co-ordinating the activities of the various industry training boards?

(a) the Department of Employment
(b) the Advisory Conciliation and Arbitration Service

(c) the Training Services Agency
(d) the Manpower Services Commission

A13 Social Security

309. What National Insurance contributions are payable by a self-employed person?

(a) Class 1 contribution
(b) Class 3 contribution
(c) Classes 2 and 4 contributions
(d) no contributions

310. Which of the following benefits is dependent upon an employee having paid a certain number of National Insurance contributions?

(a) unemployment benefit
(b) statutory sick pay (SSP)
(c) supplementary benefit
(d) family income support

311. Which of the following benefits is not available to a self-employed person?

(a) maternity allowance
(b) widow's pension
(c) unemployment benefit
(d) sickness benefit

312. A person who loses his job as a result of alleged misconduct could be disqualified from claiming unemployment benefit for a period.

(a) True
(b) False

313. To qualify for SSP an employee must be absent from work for at least:

(a) 1 complete qualifying day
(b) 2 complete qualifying days
(c) 3 complete qualifying days
(d) 4 complete qualifying days

314. The maximum entitlement for SSP in any period of incapacity for work is:

- **(a) 1 week**
- **(b) 4 weeks**
- **(c) 28 weeks**
- **(d) 52 weeks**

315. An employee who is absent from work through illness for ten days continuously, under the Statutory Sick Pay scheme must be paid sickness benefit for:

- **(a) 2 days**
- **(b) 3 days**
- **(c) 7 days**
- **(d) 10 days**

316. Under the SSP scheme an employer may claim back sickness payments:

- **(a) by deduction from his payments to the Inland Revenue**
- **(b) from the Department of Social Security**
- **(c) by deduction from the employer's National Insurance contributions to the DSS**
- **(d) from the Secretary of State for Health**

317. Under the two-tier state pension scheme an additional pension is paid according to:

- **(a) the number of years' contributions paid into the scheme**
- **(b) the length of service with the final employer**
- **(c) the total number of years in paid employment**
- **(d) the type of private pension scheme operated by the employer**

A14 Discrimination

318. Racial discrimination is not prohibited by the Race Relations Act 1976:

- **(a) in the training of employees**
- **(b) in the recruitment of company management**

(c) where employees work in private households
(d) in meeting the special educational needs of particular racial groups

319. A person subjected to racial discrimination by being refused credit sale facilities would need to complain to:

(a) the county or sheriff's court
(b) an industrial tribunal
(c) the Office of Fair Trading
(d) the Commission on Racial Equality

320. It would be lawful for an employer to pay a male employee at a higher rate than a female employee for doing the same or similar work where:

(a) the man had been employed for a longer period than the woman
(b) the man is older than the woman
(c) the man is married and the woman is single
(d) they are of different ethnic origins

321. A female employee claiming equal pay for a particular job must be able to establish that:

(a) she is a full-time employee
(b) she has been doing the particular job for at least 12 months
(c) the job she does is the same as or broadly similar to those done by the male employees
(d) her educational qualifications are equal to those of the male employees

322. An employee who feels discriminated against on the grounds of his or her sex can make a complaint to:

(a) the police
(b) the Equal Opportunities Commission
(c) an industrial tribunal
(d) the Employment Appeals Tribunal

323. Sex discrimination between the sexes is prohibited in the case of:

(a) recruitment of a matron for a girls' school

(b) recruitment of a cook to work in a private household
(c) recruitment of a telephonist/receptionist for a firm
(d) when seeking fashion models

324. A haulier could advertise under the Sex Discrimination Act for:

(a) a mature female wordprocessor operator
(b) a strong lad for warehouse duties
(c) an attractive young lady receptionist
(d) an HGV driver (male or female applicants considered)

325. Which of the following advertisements would be lawful under Sex Discrimination legislation?

(a) male washroom attendant wanted
(b) young lady wanted for typing pool
(c) warehousmen required
(d) tea lady required

326. The register of disabled persons is maintained by the:

(a) local offices of the Department of Social Security
(b) Area Health Authority
(c) Department of Employment Jobcentres
(d) Manpower Services Commission

327. Employers must employ a quota of registered disabled persons if they:

(a) employ 20 or more people
(b) employ 25 or more people
(c) are a public limited company
(d) are registered with the Manpower Services Commission

328. Employers of 20 or more persons must employ a quota of disabled people amounting to:

(a) 1 per cent of the workforce
(b) 2 per cent of the workforce
(c) 3 per cent of the workforce

(d) 5 per cent of the workforce

329. An employee may take an equal pay complaint to an industrial tribunal while still employed or within:

(a) 6 months of termination of employment
(b) 9 months of termination of employment
(c) 12 months of termination of employment
(d) an unlimited period of time

330. An employee can make a complaint to an industrial tribunal on grounds of unfair dismissal within:

(a) 1 month from the date of dismissal
(b) 2 months from the date of dismissal
(c) 3 months from the date the dismissal took effect
(d) not until 6 months have elapsed since the date of dismissal

331. An employee from a firm employing not more than 20 employees claiming for unfair dismissal to an industrial tribunal must have been employed continuously since 1985 for at least:

(a) 13 weeks
(b) 26 weeks
(c) 52 weeks
(d) 104 weeks

332. Which of the following types of employment complaint would not be dealt with by an industrial tribunal?

(a) unfair dismissal
(b) redundancy disputes
(c) complaints regarding sex discrimination
(d) claim for industrial injury benefit

A15 Safety

333. The principal object of the Factories Act is to:

(a) control the hours during which factories may operate
(b) regulate the way in which factories are built

(c) ensure the health, safety and welfare of those who work in factories
(d) lay down statutory minimum rates of pay for factory workers

334. Health and Safety at Work inspectors may enter premises as necessary to enforce the law:

(a) only if accompanied by a police officer
(b) at any time
(c) at any reasonable time
(d) only after serving a notice on the occupier 24 hours in advance

335. If a Health and Safety inspector considers that the work activities being carried out by an employer involve the immediate risk of serious personal injury to employees, the inspector may issue:

(a) a notice of intended prosecution
(b) a health and safety contravention notice
(c) an improvement notice
(d) a prohibition notice

336. When a Health and Safety inspector issues an improvement notice, the working practice to which it refers:

(a) must stop immediately until an improvement is made
(b) may continue provided the improvement is made within the specified time limit
(c) must not continue, and failure to carry out the improvement will result in prosecution
(d) may continue provided that a safety representative supervises the work

337. A fire certificate is legally required:

(a) in all works premises and offices
(b) for premises where petroleum products are used or stored
(c) if more than 20 people are employed in total or more than 10 are employed above ground floor

(d) to confirm that firms have adequate fire insurance cover

338. Safety representatives at a place of work are appointed by:

(a) the firm's managing director
(b) the company secretary
(c) the shop stewards
(d) trade union members employed in the firm

339. A person appointed as a safety representative should have been employed in that firm or in similar employment elsewhere for a minimum of:

(a) 1 year
(b) 2 years
(c) 3 years
(d) 4 years

340. Apart from domestic employees, the maximum number of persons who may be employed before a written safety policy must be produced is:

(a) 2
(b) 3
(c) 5
(d) 10

341. A qualified first-aider must be appointed when a firm employs more than:

(a) 10 people
(b) 50 people
(c) 100 people
(d) 150 people

342. In high-hazard industrial establishments a first-aid room should be provided and in premises where:

(a) more than 50 people are employed
(b) more than 100 people are employed
(c) more than 250 people are employed
(d) more than 400 people are employed

343. Where the walls of a factory or workshop have 'smooth impervious surfaces' they must be washed with hot

water and soap or cleaned by some other approved method once every:

(a) 12 months
(b) 14 months
(c) 24 months
(d) 7 years

344. Under the provisions of the Factories Act factory walls which are painted or varnished must be repainted every:

(a) 14 months
(b) 5 years
(c) 7 years
(d) 10 years

345. Where a substantial amount of work in a work room involves sitting down and requires little physical effort, the temperature after the first hour must be not less than:

(a) 15 degrees Centigrade
(b) 16 degrees Centigrade
(c) 18 degrees Centigrade
(d) 66 degrees Fahrenheit

346. The Factories Act requires air receivers to be examined by a competent person once every:

(a) 6 months
(b) 12 months
(c) 24 months
(d) 26 months

347. The Factories Act requires cranes used in industrial premises to be examined by a competent person once every:

(a) 6 months
(b) 12 months
(c) 14 months
(d) 18 months

348. The Factories Act specifies minimum numbers of separate toilet facilities for male and female employees.

How many toilets would need to be provided where there are 75 male employees and two female employees?

(a) 4 male plus 1 female
(b) 4 male plus 2 female
(c) 2 male plus 2 female
(d) 4 male plus 2 female and 1 for visitors

349. Where a serious work accident falls within the scope of the RIDDOR regulations this has to be reported:

(a) immediately by telephone
(b) immediately by telephone followed in writing within 7 days
(c) in writing within 7 days
(d) only if the injured person subsequently dies

350. Reports on accidents involving death or injury during loading, unloading or the conveyance of dangerous chemicals must be made to:

(a) the police
(b) the Goods Vehicle Licensing Authority
(c) the Health and Safety Executive
(d) the Department of Health

5: Typical Questions – National Examination Module B: Goods Syllabus only

B1 Drivers' Hours

351. The maximum time that a driver engaged on UK domestic work can be on duty in one week is:

(a) 48 hours
(b) 55 hours
(c) 60 hours
(d) 77 hours

352. Under EC regulations the maximum aggregated driving permitted before a statutory break must be taken is:

(a) 4 hours
(b) 4.5 hours
(c) 5 hours
(d) 8 hours

353. EC regulation 3820/85, which limits driving to a normal maximum of 9 hours daily, permits an extension to:

(a) 10 hours on 2 days in any 7-day period
(b) 10 hours on any 2 days in a week
(c) 11 hours on 2 days in a week if the extra time is compensated
(d) 13 hours on 2 days so long as 11-hours' daily rest is taken

354. The maximum time that a driver can spend behind the wheel in any one week under EC rules is:

(a) 36 hours

(b) 54 hours
(c) 60 hours
(d) 6 daily driving shifts

355. If a driver spends 45 hours behind the wheel in one week under EC rules, how many hours can he spend driving during the next following fixed week?

(a) 34 hours
(b) 45 hours
(c) 54 hours
(d) 56 hours

356. Under EC Regulation 3820/85 a driver is restricted to a 2-weekly driving limit of:

(a) 90 hours
(b) 92 hours
(c) 102 hours
(d) 104 hours

357. Current EC rules restrict the maximum working time for a 2-man vehicle crew by setting a minimum rest period requirement of:

(a) 10 hours each in 27 hours
(b) 8 hours each in 30 hours
(c) 11 hours each in 24 hours
(d) 22 hours between them

358. Under EC Regulation 3820/85 the driver's statutory minimum break period may be spread throughout the driving period and taken as other breaks of:

(a) at least 20 minutes each
(b) at least 30 minutes each
(c) at least 45 minutes each
(d) at least 15 minutes each

359. If a driver of a vehicle within the scope of the EC rules starts work at 8.00am and drives continuously until 12.30pm he must then

(a) take a break of 20 minutes
(b) take a single break of half an hour and another break later that day

(c) take a single break of three-quarters of an hour
(d) take a break of 20 minutes with two further breaks of 20 minutes each

360. A driver starting a journey at 6.00am takes a 15-minute break at 8.00am then continues driving. To comply with Community rules he must take a further 30 minute break at:

(a) 10.30am
(b) 10.45am
(c) 11.00am
(d) 11.45am

361. A driver came on duty at 07.00 hours, loaded his vehicle, and at 08.30 commenced his journey. Under current EC regulations, if he drives continuously he must take a 45-minute break starting not later than:

(a) 11.30 hours
(b) 12.30 hours
(c) 13.00 hours
(d) 14.00 hours

362. EC regulations permit a driver to replace the 45-minute mandatory break with:

(a) 2 breaks of at least 15 minutes each during the driving period
(b) 3 breaks of at least 15 minutes each taken during the day
(c) 3 breaks of at least 20 minutes each
(d) other breaks of at least 15 minutes each totalling 45 minutes

363. Provisions in the Community drivers' hours rules allow national exemption for vehicles operating exclusively on islands having an area not exceeding:

(a) 1,000 square miles
(b) 2,000 square kilometres
(c) 2,300 square kilometres
(d) 2,300 square miles

364. Emergency provisions in the Community rules permit a driver in given circumstances to depart from:

(a) the daily and weekly driving limits only
(b) both daily and weekly rest period requirements
(c) both driving limits and rest period requirements
(d) none of the statutory driving or rest period requirements

365. Which of the following goods vehicles is subject to drivers' hours rules under EC Regulation 3820/85?

(a) a vehicle with a maximum permissible weight of 3.5 tonnes
(b) a vehicle with a maximum permissible weight exceeding 3.5 tonnes
(c) a gas board vehicle with a maximum permissible weight of 7.5 tonnes
(d) a vehicle used for milk collection from farms

366. A driver of a goods vehicle with a permissible maximum weight of 7.5 tonnes, when driving within the UK is subject to:

(a) the national drivers' hours rules
(b) the British domestic drivers' hours rules
(c) the EC drivers' hours rules
(d) no limit on his driving times

367. A 'day' for the purposes of the EC drivers' hours rules is defined as:

(a) the period from midnight to midnight
(b) a period of 24 hours counted from the time of clocking on
(c) a period of 24 hours preceding any time spent driving
(d) any period of 24 hours

368. A 'week' for the purposes of the EC drivers' hours rules is defined as:

(a) any period of seven consecutive working days
(b) the period from 00.00 on Monday to 24.00 on the following Sunday
(c) from midnight Sunday until midnight on the following Sunday

(d) any consecutive 6-day period during which a driver works

369. The normal minimum daily rest requirement under EC rules is:

(a) 10 hours
(b) 11 hours
(c) 12 hours
(d) 13 hours

370. The minimum uninterrupted period which may be counted as daily rest under EC rules is:

(a) 15 minutes
(b) 30 minutes
(c) 1 hour
(d) 2 hours

371. For the past week a driver has taken the full 11-hour daily rest period. On a 2-day journey away from base he may take a daily rest period of not less than:

(a) 8 hours
(b) 9 hours
(c) 10 hours
(d) 11 hours

372. EC Regulation 3820/85 requires the driver of a double-manned vehicle to have a minimum daily rest period of at least:

(a) 27 hours
(b) 8 hours in the past 30 hours
(c) 9 hours in the past 30 hours
(d) 8 hours in the past 27 hours

373. When a daily rest period under EC rules is not reduced it may be split into two or three periods, one of which must be at least:

(a) 6 hours
(b) 7 hours
(c) 8 hours
(d) 9 hours

374. Under EC rules daily rest periods may be reduced to:

(a) 9 hours on 3 occasions in a week
(b) 9 hours on 2 occasions in 7 days
(c) 8 hours on 3 occasions in a week
(d) 8 hours on 2 occasions in 7 days

375. When reduced daily rest periods have been taken on 2 occasions in the current week these reductions must be compensated:

(a) in the same week
(b) by the end of the next following week
(c) before the end of the third following week
(d) before the end of the fourth following week

376. Compensated daily and weekly rest periods must be attached to other rest periods of at least:

(a) 11 hours
(b) 10 hours
(c) 9 hours
(d) 8 hours

377. Which of the following vehicles would be exempt from EC rules and subject to British domestic rules?

(a) a vehicle having a permissible maximum weight of 3.5 tonnes
(b) vehicle having a permissible maximum weight of 7.5 tonnes
(c) a vehicle having a maximum permissible weight of 2.5 tonnes towing a trailer with a permissible maximum weight of 1,500kg
(d) a vehicle having a permissible maximum weight of 3 tonnes towing a trailer with a permissible maximum weight of 600kg

378. Under British domestic rules a driver is permitted to drive for a maximum daily period of:

(a) 10 hours
(b) 11 hours
(c) 12 hours
(d) 12.5 hours

379. **If a driver operating under British domestic rules finishes an 11-hour duty shift at 6.00pm, what is the earliest time he can start work the next day?**

(a) 4.00am
(b) 5.00am
(c) 6.00am
(d) 7.00am

380. **A driver employed solely on British domestic work is restricted to a maximum time on duty in any working week of:**

(a) 54 hours
(b) 60 hours
(c) 77 hours
(d) 92 hours

381. **Under the British domestic drivers' hours regulations, 'driving' means:**

(a) time spent with the engine running and the vehicle in motion
(b) time spent with the vehicle in motion and carrying a load
(c) time spent at the wheel with the engine running whether the vehicle is moving or not
(d) time spent between starting and finishing work for the day

382. **A medical practitioner using a van for professional purposes under the British domestic driver's hours regulations is subject to:**

(a) daily duty limits only
(b) daily driving limits only
(c) both daily duty and daily driving limits
(d) no limits on his daily driving and duty times

B2 Record Keeping

383. **If a delivery vehicle under 3.5 tonnes maximum permissible weight does not need an 'O' licence, what record-keeping requirements apply to the driver?**

(a) he must use a tachograph to produce records
(b) he must use a domestic driver's record book
(c) he must keep a note of his driving on a time sheet
(d) he is not legally required to keep records

384. A driver of a vehicle exempt from the EC rules must complete a record sheet even though he drives for only 3 hours on each day of the week.

(a) True
(b) False

385. When an employee-driver keeping 'domestic' records changes jobs, to whom must he return his record book?

(a) the Licensing Authority
(b) he must keep it himself for at least 12 months
(c) his new employer
(d) the employer who issued it

386. Written records need not be kept by drivers engaged on British domestic operations who, on any day, do not drive for more than 4 hours and who do not drive outside a radius from the vehicle operating centre of:

(a) 30 miles
(b) 35 kilometres
(c) 50 kilometres
(d) 50 miles

387. A driver must retain his completed domestic record book for at least:

(a) 2 days
(b) 7 days
(c) 14 days
(d) 1 month

388. Drivers using weekly record books under the domestic rules must return them to their employer for examination and signature within:

(a) 5 days
(b) 7 days
(c) 10 days

(d) 14 days

389. Employers are required to keep completed record books and duplicate daily record sheets for at least:

(a) 6 months
(b) 9 months
(c) 12 months
(d) 15 months

390. For which of the following vehicles does EC law require drivers to make statutory records of their hours of work?

(a) those not exceeding 3.5 tonnes gross plated weight
(b) those exceeding 3.5 tonnes maximum permissible weight
(c) those under 1,525kg unladen weight
(d) all vehicles except those of the fire, police and military services

391. Where a driver drives more than one goods vehicle during his day's work, he must complete one tachograph chart:

(a) for each vehicle driven that day
(b) for the vehicle driven for the longest period in the day
(c) for the first vehicle driven that day
(d) if practicable, to cover all the vehicles driven in the day

392. When completing a daily tachograph chart the driver should:

(a) record the exact time at which any vehicle changeover took place
(b) record the time of changeover to the nearest 15 minutes
(c) record the time of changeover to the nearest 30 minutes
(d) record just the relevant vehicle registration numbers

393. A motor fitter driving a vehicle which falls within EC Regulation 3821/85 on a local road test after repair must complete a tachograph chart.

(a) True
(b) False

394. When commencing a day's work an HGV driver must enter which of the following information in the centre field of his tachograph chart?

(a) the time at which he commenced the shift
(b) the name and address of his employer
(c) the place from which he commenced his day's journey
(d) the amount of daily rest taken prior to commencing the shift

395. If a tachograph chart is damaged while in use by the driver:

(a) it must be attached to the chart used to replace it
(b) it must be retained by the driver for at least 21 days
(c) it can be destroyed or retained by the driver as he wishes
(d) it must be returned to the employer as soon as is reasonably possible

396. A tachograph instrument must be installed so that when opened, but without removing the chart, the recordings can be read for the previous:

(a) 6 hours
(b) 8 hours
(c) 9 hours
(d) 10 hours

397. A broad black trace made on a tachograph chart indicates that:

(a) the vehicle is moving
(b) the engine is running while the vehicle is standing
(c) the tachograph face is not properly closed

(d) the driver has turned the mode switch to record driving

398. With a 2-man tachograph, the chart for the non-driving crew member will show recordings of:

(a) distance and activity mode only
(b) speed and distance only
(c) speed, activity mode, distance and time
(d) activity mode and time only

399. Drivers are required to keep tachograph charts with them, and available for inspection by the enforcement authorities, for:

(a) the current week only
(b) the current week plus the previous week
(c) the current week plus the last day of the previous driving week
(d) the current week plus the last 2 days of the previous week

400. Completed tachograph charts must be returned to the employer no later than:

(a) 7 days after use
(b) 12 days after use
(c) 14 days after use
(d) 21 days after use

401. Tachograph charts must be retained by the operator and kept available for inspection, if required, by the enforcement authorities for at least:

(a) 12 months
(b) 15 months
(c) 21 months
(d) 24 months

402. A driver who is unavoidably delayed on a journey and has exceeded the EC drivers' hours limits must:

(a) notify the DTp Traffic Area office with details as soon as possible
(b) report the facts to the police as soon as possible

(c) enter the details on his tachograph chart for that day
(d) report the circumstances to an enforcement officer within 24 hours

403. Under EC regulations, a calibrated tachograph installation must be fitted to which of the following vehicles?

(a) a goods vehicle with a permissible maximum weight of 5 tonnes used only in the UK
(b) a local authority refuse collection vehicle with a permissible maximum weight of 10 tonnes
(c) a delivery vehicle with a permissible maximum weight of 2 tonnes used only in national road transport operations
(d) a goods vehicle with a permissible maximum weight of 3.5 tonnes used for national and international journeys

404. When presenting an articulated vehicle to an approved tachograph centre for tachograph calibration, only the tractive unit is needed for this purpose.

(a) True
(b) False

405. When a newly installed tachograph is first calibrated the vehicle must be:

(a) unladen
(b) fully loaded
(c) loaded above 3.5 tonnes gross weight
(d) standing on a gradient of less than 16 per cent

406. Responsibility for ensuring that the tachograph installed in a vehicle functions correctly at all times rests with:

(a) the driver only
(b) the vehicle operator only
(c) both the driver and the operator
(d) the vehicle owner

407. The law requires tachographs to be re-calibrated at approved centres in the United Kingdom every:

(a) 1 year
(b) 2 years
(c) 3 years
(d) 6 years

408. The speed recording mechanism in a tachograph must be accurate 'in use' to within:

(a) plus or minus 6 kilometres per hour at speeds in excess of 10kph
(b) plus or minus 6 kilometres per hour at all speeds
(c) 10 per cent at speeds above 10mph
(d) plus or minus 10 per cent all speeds

409. A new 'plaque' must be fitted to the tachograph after re-calibration every:

(a) 6 years
(b) 3 years
(c) 2 years
(d) 1 year

410. Tachograph 'checks' must be carried out by a DTp approved fitter or workshop at least every:

(a) 5 years
(b) 4 years
(c) 3 years
(d) 2 years

411. Responsibility for ensuring that seals on the connections between the tachograph head and the gearbox remain intact on a goods vehicle rests with:

(a) the vehicle operator only
(b) the driver only
(c) both the operator and the driver
(d) the installation fitter or workshop

412. If a tachograph becomes unserviceable during a journey, it must be repaired en route if the vehicle is unable to return to base within a maximum of:

(a) 2 days
(b) 2 weeks

(c) 1 week
(d) 10 days

413. Which of the following officials has legal authority to inspect a goods vehicle driver's records of hours of work:

(a) a traffic warden
(b) a public health inspector
(c) a Customs officer
(d) a police officer in uniform

414. A DTp examiner or a uniformed police officer may enter premises to inspect drivers' and vehicle records:

(a) at any time with the owner's permission
(b) at any reasonable time
(c) only during working hours
(d) after giving 48 hours notice

415. Police have statutory powers to enter premises to inspect drivers' records:

(a) only between 9.00am and 5.00pm
(b) at any reasonable time
(c) at any time with the owner's consent
(d) they have no such powers

416. An enforcement officer may legally demand the production of tachograph records at a specified Traffic Area office within a period of:

(a) 3 days
(b) 5 days
(c) 7 days
(d) 10 days

417. Which of the following penalties could be imposed on a vehicle operator by a Licensing Authority for contravention of the drivers' hours rules?

(a) up to six months' imprisonment
(b) a fine of up to £250
(c) endorsement of his ordinary licence
(d) revocation, suspension or curtailment of the 'O' licence

B3 HGV Driving Licences

418. **Heavy goods vehicle driving licences are currently issued by:**

(a) the Licensing Authority at Traffic Area offices
(b) the Driver and Vehicle Licensing Centre, Swansea
(c) main post offices
(d) local licensing offices

419. **HGV drivers' licences are issued from the Traffic Area in which:**

(a) the applicant works
(b) the applicant's employer has his operating centre
(c) the applicant lives
(d) the applicant was born

420. **A medical certificate must accompany the first application for an HGV driving licence and renewals made after the applicant reaches the age of:**

(a) 46 years
(b) 60 years
(c) 62 years
(d) 65 years

421. **Which of the following vehicles are exempt from the need for the driver to hold an HGV driving licence?**

(a) goods vehicles operating under a trade licence
(b) public service vehicles
(c) goods vehicles not exceeding 10 tonnes maximum permissible weight
(d) an articulated tractive unit not exceeding 7.5 tonnes unladen with no semi-trailer attached

422. **An application for an HGV licence can be made ahead of the date required but not exceeding a period of:**

(a) 1 month
(b) 2 months
(c) 4 weeks
(d) 3 months

423. **HGV driving licence applicants must declare any convictions for hours and records, loading and vehicle roadworthiness offences during:**

(a) the past 4 years
(b) the past 5 years
(c) the past 7 years
(d) the past 10 years

424. For the purposes of driver licensing which of the following is classified as a 'small goods vehicle'?

(a) a goods vehicle with a maximum permissible weight of 6.5 tonnes drawing a trailer of 2 tonnes
(b) a goods vehicle with a maximum permissible weight of 7 tonnes drawing a trailer of 1 tonne
(c) a goods vehicle with a maximum permissible weight of 7 tonnes drawing a trailer of 2 tonnes
(d) a goods vehicle with a maximum permissible weight of 2.5 tonnes drawing a trailer of 1 tonne

425. A learner HGV driver holding both provisional HGV and ordinary licences must display on the front and rear of the vehicle:

(a) an HGV 'L' plate only
(b) an ordinary 'L' plate only
(c) both HGV and ordinary 'L' plates
(d) a driver training school plate

426. A learner passing the HGV driving test while holding both provisional ordinary and HGV driving licences will gain a certificate of competence to drive HGVs of the type on which the test was taken and vehicles of Group A or B.

(a) True
(b) False

427. The holder of provisional ordinary and HGV Class III driving licences must comply with which of the following conditions for provisional licence holders?

(a) he is not allowed to drive on a motorway
(b) he can drive a 6-wheel vehicle
(c) he can drive a 4-wheel rigid vehicle towing a drawbar trailer
(d) he can drive an articulated tractive unit with automatic transmission

428. When a broken-down heavy goods vehicle is being towed on a rigid towbar the person steering it must hold:

(a) a full ordinary driving licence
(b) an HGV driving licence of the appropriate class
(c) both an ordinary driving licence and a correct HGV driving licence
(d) a driving licence is not needed for this purpose

429. If the driver of a heavy goods vehicle is taken ill while driving on a motorway and is unable to continue his journey:

(a) he must struggle on to the next service area to get help
(b) the vehicle may be driven to safety by a police officer even though he may not hold the correct class of HGV driving licence
(c) the vehicle owner must send a replacement driver to remove it
(d) it can only be moved by an AA/RAC patrolman with an HGV licence

430. In order to take the HGV driving test a person must hold:

(a) a provisional ordinary driving licence only
(b) a provisional HGV driving licence only
(c) a full ordinary driving licence only
(d) both a provisional or a full ordinary driving licence and a provisional HGV driving licence

431. The minimum age at which a driver may drive an articulated vehicle (where the tractive unit exceeds 2 tonnes unladen) on the public highway is:

(a) 17 years
(b) 18 years
(c) 21 years
(d) 25 years

432. The minimum age at which a person can drive a goods vehicle with a maximum permissible weight of 3 tonnes is:

(a) 17 years
(b) 18 years
(c) 19 years
(d) 21 years

433. Where a goods vehicle exceeds 3.5 tonnes but not 7.5 tonnes maximum permissible weight the driver must be aged at least:

(a) 16 years
(b) 17 years
(c) 18 years
(d) 21 years

434. The holder of a Class III restricted HGV driving licence is limited to driving vehicles with a maximum weight not exceeding:

(a) 7 tonnes
(b) 7.5 tonnes
(c) 10 tonnes
(d) 16 tonnes

435. A Class III HGV licence holder learning to drive vehicles of Class II would need to be accompanied by the holder of a current HGV driving licence of:

(a) Class I
(b) Class II
(c) Class III
(d) Class IIIA

436. Where employee drivers hold HGV driving licences of Class IIA, ideally replacement vehicles should be of which of the following types?

(a) articulated with automatic transmission and tractive units not exceeding 2 tonnes unladen weight
(b) articulated with automatic transmission and tractive units exceeding 2 tonnes unladen weight
(c) heavy rigids with automatic transmission with more than 4 wheels
(d) heavy rigids not with automatic transmission and more than 4 wheels

437. The holder of a Class III HGV driving licence may drive a 2-axle articulated tractive unit with no trailer attached.

(a) True
(b) False

438. To apply to join the young HGV driver training scheme a trainee must possess a full ordinary driving licence free from endorsements.

(a) True
(b) False

439. Which of the following bodies is not represented on the national joint training committee for the young HGV driver training scheme?

(a) Training Services Agency
(b) National Union of Railwaymen
(c) Freight Transport Association
(d) Department of Employment

440. A 20-year-old trainee driver who passes the Class 1 HGV driving test may:

(a) drive articulated heavy goods vehicles unsupervised
(b) drive articulated heavy goods vehicles under supervision
(c) drive large goods vehicles drawing a trailer unsupervised
(d) not drive an articulated heavy goods vehicle until he is aged 21 years

441. When a Licensing Authority revokes an HGV driving licence the holder can appeal to:

(a) the Secretary of State for Transport
(b) the Transport Tribunal
(c) a magistrates' court
(d) the High Court

442. A driver whose HGV driving licence has been suspended by a Licensing Authority can appeal against the decision, first direct to the LA and then to:

(a) a magistrates' court
(b) the county court
(c) the Court of Appeal
(d) the Transport Tribunal

443. To which of the following persons is a driver legally required to produce his HGV driving licence on demand?

(a) a goods vehicle examiner
(b) a lorry park attendant
(c) a Customs and Excise officer
(d) a person whose car he has damaged

444. If a Department of Transport authorised examiner demands production of an HGV driver's licence, the law allows the driver to produce it:

(a) at a police station named by the driver within 5 days
(b) at the office of the examiner or the Licensing Authority within 5 days
(c) at the office of the examiner or the Licensing Authority within 10 days
(d) at any nominated police station within 10 days

B4 Goods Vehicle Speed Limits

445. On motorways, dual-purpose vehicles are limited to a maximum speed of:

(a) 40mph
(b) 50mph
(c) 60mph
(d) 70mph

446. The maximum permitted speed for a goods vehicle not exceeding 7.5 tonnes mlw and drawing a trailer is:

(a) 60mph
(b) 50mph
(c) 40mph
(d) 30mph

447. The maximum permitted speed for a van with a gross weight of 3,550kg on a single carriageway road is:

(a) 30mph
(b) 40mph
(c) 50mph
(d) 60mph

448. The maximum permitted speed for a van with an unladen weight of 1,200kg on a single carriageway road is:

(a) 30mph
(b) 40mph
(c) 50mph
(d) 60mph

449. A rigid goods vehicle not exceeding 7,500kg mlw may travel on motorways at a maximum speed of:

(a) 70mph
(b) 60mph
(c) 50mph
(d) 40mph

450. The speed limit for a vehicle with a maximum laden weight not exceeding 7.5 tonnes and towing a trailer on a dual carriageway road is:

(a) 30mph
(b) 40mph
(c) 50mph
(d) 60mph

451. Which of the following categories of vehicle is restricted to 60 mph on motorways?

(a) rigid goods vehicles over 7.5 tonnes mlw
(b) vehicles designed to carry not more than 8 passengers
(c) dual-purpose vehicles
(d) rigid goods vehicles not exceeding 1,525kg unladen

452. The maximum permitted speed on a motorway for a goods vehicle with a maximum laden weight of 12,000kg and towing a drawbar trailer is:

(a) 30mph
(b) 40mph
(c) 50mph
(d) 60mph

453. The maximum permitted speed on a dual carriageway for a rigid 8-wheel vehicle is:

(a) 30mph
(b) 40mph
(c) 50mph
(d) 60mph

454. The maximum permitted speed for an articulated vehicle exceeding 7.5 tonnes maximum laden weight on an ordinary de-restricted road is:

(a) 30mph
(b) 40mph
(c) 50mph
(d) 60mph

455. Works trucks are restricted to a maximum speed of:

(a) 18mph
(b) 15mph
(c) 20mph
(d) 30mph

456. Special types vehicles of Category III carrying a load are restricted to a maximum speed on motorways of:

(a) 12mph
(b) 15mph
(c) 20mph
(d) 30mph

B5 Accident Procedure

457. In which of the following accidents involving injury to animals must the driver stop and give particulars to the police or other persons with reasonable grounds for requiring them?

(a) where there is injury to a deer
(b) where there is injury to a pig carried in the vehicle
(c) where there is injury to a goat
(d) where there is injury to a goose

458. The driver of a motor vehicle involved in a road accident is required by law to:

(a) obtain the assistance of a police officer
(b) place warning triangles on the road near the accident scene
(c) stop and give particulars to any person reasonably requiring them
(d) take adequate steps to protect people from further risks

459. If a driver was not aware at the time that his vehicle had been involved in an accident, he may not be convicted for failing to stop and report it.

(a) True
(b) False

460. If after stopping at an injury accident in which he is involved, the driver does not give necessary information to a police officer or other person having reasonable grounds for requiring it, he must report to the police:

(a) within 24 hours
(b) as soon as possible but in any case not later than 24 hours afterwards
(c) within 5 days
(d) immediately

461. Road accidents should normally be reported to the vehicle insurers:

(a) only if a claim is to be made
(b) at the earliest opportunity
(c) within 24 hours
(d) within 7 days

462. When involved in a personal injury accident where the police take details at the scene, the driver is not required at that time to:

(a) give his name and address
(b) give the vehicle owner's name and address
(c) give the vehicle registration number
(d) produce the vehicle insurance certificate

463. Following a road accident the term 'third party' refers to:

(a) the insurance company
(b) the other party involved
(c) the owner of the vehicle
(d) an eye witness

464. A motor vehicle owner who was not driving at the time his vehicle was involved in a road accident:

(a) must tell the police who was the driver if they intend prosecuting for a road traffic offence
(b) must tell the police who was the driver if there was personal injury
(c) must in any case tell the police the driver's identity if known
(d) has no legal liability to tell the police who was the driver

465. At the scene of a road accident where there are no personal injuries a driver is required by law to:

(a) give details from his driving licence
(b) produce his insurance policy for examination
(c) give the serial number of his certificate of insurance to any witness
(d) give his name and address to any person reasonably requiring it

466. A driver has a legal responsibility to stop at the scene of a road accident:

(a) if he runs over a chicken
(b) if he runs over a stray cat
(c) if he injures only himself in the accident
(d) if he injures a dog

467. If legally required information was not given at the scene of a road accident involving personal injury or damage this must be reported to the police:

(a) by the driver by telephone
(b) by the driver in writing
(c) by a witness
(d) by the driver in person

468. Which of the following constitutes a legally reportable road traffic accident?

(a) where only the driver of the vehicle involved is injured
(b) where sheep being carried on the vehicle involved are injured
(c) where a passenger being carried in the vehicle involved is injured
(d) where the driver of a vehicle knocks down and kills a cat

469. What information must a driver involved in a road traffic accident give to the driver of any other vehicle involved?

(a) his destination
(b) details from his driving licence
(c) the name and address of the vehicle owner
(d) the name and address of the vehicle owner's insurance company

470. Under the Road Traffic Act 1988, section 170, which of the following constitutes a reportable road traffic accident?

(a) running over and killing a goose
(b) colliding with another vehicle but causing no damage
(c) colliding with and damaging a wooden fence adjacent to the road
(d) the driver accidentally trapping a passenger's hand in the door

471. If a lorry collides with a stationary car damaging it but causing no personal injury, and the lorry driver, although aware of the accident, does not stop at the scene but reports the matter to the police 2 hours later:

(a) he commits no offence because the accident was reported to the police within 24 hours
(b) he commits an offence because he did not stop at the scene of the accident
(c) he does not commit an offence because no person was injured
(d) he commits no offence because the car was parked illegally blocking a delivery entrance

B6 Vehicle Insurance and Carrier's Liability

472. The basic legal requirement for compulsory third-party vehicle insurance is currently set out in:

(a) the Road Vehicles (Construction and Use) Regulations 1986
(b) the Highways Act 1980
(c) the Road Traffic Offenders Act 1988
(d) the Road Traffic Act 1988

473. Which of the following motor vehicles are exempt from the requirement for compulsory third-party insurance cover?

(a) goods vehicles being operated under a trade licence
(b) vehicles operated by a county or district council in England and Wales
(c) vehicles travelling to or from a place to be tested
(d) vehicles operated by a person who is non-resident in the UK

474. An insurance company offering motor insurance in compliance with legal requirements must be:

(a) a member of a Lloyds insurance syndicate
(b) a member of the Motor Insurers' Bureau
(c) approved by the Department of Trade and Industry
(d) approved by the Insurance Ombudsman

475. To avoid any resulting liabilities a passenger can legally agree with the driver to travel in a vehicle entirely at his own risk.

(a) True
(b) False

476. Insurance cover provided by a certificate of motor insurance becomes valid:

(a) 24 hours after the certificate has been issued
(b) when the certificate is in the post to the insured
(c) only when the insured has the certificate in his possession
(d) from the time the insured telephones vehicle details to the insurers

477. A certificate of motor insurance must contain details of:

(a) the persons authorised to drive vehicles covered by the policy
(b) the premiums paid on the policy
(c) whether excise duty has been paid on vehicles covered by the policy
(d) whether the vehicles covered are the subject of a hire purchase agreement

478. The legal requirement for a vehicle owner to pay for emergency hospital treatment for persons injured in a road traffic accident involving his vehicle would be covered by his:

(a) fidelity guarantee insurance
(b) consequential loss insurance
(c) third-party motor insurance
(d) employer's liability insurance

479. For which of the following offences could a goods vehicle operator be held liable by a court although he was not driving the vehicle concerned at the time the offence was committed?

(a) failure to hold third-party insurance cover for the vehicle
(b) failure to stop following a road accident
(c) failure to comply with traffic directions
(d) failure to give particulars at the scene of an accident

480. If a driver cannot produce a certificate of insurance when requested to do so by a police officer, it must be produced at a police station:

(a) personally within 24 hours
(b) personally within 3 days
(c) personally within 5 days
(d) personally or by somebody on his behalf within 7 days

481. If a vehicle not covered by third-party insurance knocks down a pedestrian, a lamp-post and a garden wall, who can successfully claim compensation under the Motor Insurers' Bureau scheme?

(a) the pedestrian only
(b) the owner of the lamp-post
(c) the owner of the garden wall
(d) the pedestrian, the owners of the lamp-post and the garden wall

482. If an employee driver is charged with driving a vehicle while not insured against third-party risks, he has a valid defence if he can prove the vehicle was not his and he had no reason to believe it was not insured.

(a) True
(b) False

483. In addition to third-party motor insurance, for which of the following is a vehicle operator required by law to have insurance cover?

(a) passenger liability
(b) damage to his own vehicles
(c) fire
(d) theft of his own vehicles

484. As an alternative to normal third-party cover taken out with an insurance company a vehicle owner may deposit a sum of money as security with:

(a) the Supreme Court
(b) the Secretary of State for Transport
(c) a Chief Constable of police

(d) the Home Office

485. An organisation wishing to carry its own third-party motor insurance risks may do so, provided it deposits with the Accountant General of the Supreme Court as security the sum of:

(a) £15,000
(b) £20,000
(c) £25,000
(d) £50,000

486. A road haulier can restrict his legal liability by defining the limits of his liability in his:

(a) articles of association
(b) memorandum of association
(c) contracts of employment
(d) conditions of carriage

487. By accepting haulage contracts subject to the terms laid down in his conditions of carriage, an operator restricts his legal liability to that of:

(a) a public carrier
(b) a common carrier
(c) a corporate carrier
(d) a private carrier

B7 Safe Loading of Vehicles and Transit of Goods

488. The legal requirement for the safe loading of vehicles is contained in:

(a) the Goods Vehicles (Operators' Licences, Qualifications and Fees) Regulations 1984
(b) the Carriage of Goods by Road Act 1965
(c) the Goods Vehicles (Ascertainment of Maximum Gross Weights) Regulations 1976
(d) the Road Vehicles (Construction and Use) Regulations 1986

489. The DTp 'Safety of Loads' Code of Practice states that rope used for load lashing should be at least:

(a) 3 strand and minimum 10mm nominal diameter
(b) 3 strand and minimum 12mm nominal diameter
(c) 3 strand and minimum 15 mm nominal diameter
(d) 5 strand and minimum 10mm nominal diameter

490. The DTp Code of Practice on the safe loading of vehicles states that to prevent movement of the load in a forward direction, a load restraint device should be capable of withstanding a force equal to:

(a) half the total weight of the load
(b) three-quarters of the total weight of the load
(c) the full weight of the load
(d) twice the full weight of the load

491. The legal requirements on load safety are that vehicle operators must:

(a) use only approved webbing straps and tensioners for securing loads
(b) ensure that all loads are secure and not likely to cause danger
(c) use only British Standards approved load restraint systems
(d) follow the guidelines in the DTp Code of Practice on load safety

492. If a heavy goods vehicle is found by the police to be overloaded, prosecution and likely conviction for this offence will rest with:

(a) the driver only
(b) the driver's employer only
(c) both the driver and his employer
(d) the vehicle loaders

493. If a load shifts or falls from a heavy goods vehicle, who is liable to prosecution for an insecure load?

(a) the driver only
(b) the driver's employer
(c) both the driver and his employer
(d) the vehicle loaders

494. While travelling on a road, part of a load falls from a vehicle when a faulty rope breaks. What legal action will follow?

(a) if the driver was not aware of the fault in the rope he is not liable
(b) there is no defence against using a vehicle with an insecure load
(c) liability rests with the loader not the driver
(d) as the rope breakage was accidental no offence has been committed

495. Which authority in the UK is responsible for making and enforcing the regulations relating to the carriage of dangerous substances by road?

(a) the police
(b) the Health and Safety Executive
(c) the Department of Transport
(d) the Department of Trade and Industry

496. The Dangerous Substances (Carriage by Road in Road Tankers and Tank Containers) Regulations 1981 define a tank container as one which has a cubic capacity exceeding:

(a) 1 cubic metre
(b) 2 cubic metres
(c) 3 cubic metres
(d) 5 cubic metres

497. A haulier must be provided with information in writing when collecting a tanker load of dangerous substance covered by the HSE 'Approved List'. The information required details:

(a) the risks to health and safety created by the substance
(b) the name of the original manufacturer of the substance
(c) the location of safe parking areas en route
(d) the individual chemical constitutents of the substance

498. The Road Traffic (Carriage of Dangerous Substances in Packages etc.) Regulations 1986 do not apply when carrying medium risk substances if:

(a) no more than 32 gallons is conveyed in metal drums
(b) they are conveyed in containers not exceeding 5 litres
(c) they are conveyed in containers not exceeding 200 litres
(d) they are conveyed in containers not exceeding 250 litres

499. Information concerning a dangerous substance being carried by road is usually carried in the form of a Tremcard, which is a document to be:

(a) carried on the vehicle at all times when it is loaded with dangerous substances
(b) shown to the police for every district through which the vehicle passes
(c) given to the Fire Brigade in case they are called to deal with an emergency situation
(d) produced by the driver as evidence of his training in the handling of dangerous substances

500. Which of the following legal requirements do not generally have to be met when dangerous substances are carried by road?

(a) a suitable and efficient fire extinguisher must be carried
(b) employees must be made aware of and comply with appropriate regulations
(c) details of movements must be advised to the police and highway authorities
(d) steps must be taken to ensure that none of the substance is spilt

501. Road tankers carrying a flammable substance on a journey within the UK must display an approved flame symbol which is:

(a) red on a black background
(b) black on a red background
(c) black on a orange reflective background
(d) luminous orange on a black matt background

502. **A hazardous warning label displayed on a road tanker carrying a multi-load of dangerous substances must contain:**

- (a) identification labels for all the substances carried
- (b) a list of all the individual substances carried
- (c) the word 'multi-load'
- (d) the names of the manufacturers of each of the substances

503. **Hazardous warning notices on tanker vehicles show 2 sets of letters or numbers, the lower set with a 4-digit number being the substance identification number while the upper set is:**

- (a) the emergency action code
- (b) the substance name or code number
- (c) a flammable symbol
- (d) an emergency contact telephone number

504. **Road tankers carrying listed dangerous substances are required to display a rectangular warning notice giving details including:**

- (a) the destination of the load
- (b) the emergency service to be notified in case of accident
- (c) the place where the vehicle was loaded
- (d) the emergency action code for the particular substance

505. **Which of the following vehicles can be driven across a half-barrier level crossing without first obtaining permission from the signalman?**

- (a) a vehicle exceeding 38 tonnes maximum permissible weight
- (b) a vehicle exceeding 9ft 6in in width
- (c) a vehicle exceeding 48ft in length
- (d) a vehicle incapable of exceeding 5mph

506. **A load 25.5 metres long may be carried on a standard vehicle provided that:**

- (a) 2 days' notice is given to the police for every district through which it is to pass

(b) a statutory attendant is carried
(c) prior approval is obtained from the Secretary of State for Transport
(d) legal requirements for the display of marker boards are observed

507. When moving abnormal indivisible loads, if the total weight of the vehicle and its load exceeds 80,000kgs the road and bridge authorities concerned must be given:

(a) 2 clear working days' notice
(b) 3 clear working days' notice
(c) 5 clear working days' notice
(d) 6 clear working days' notice

508. Five clear days' notice in prescribed form must be given to every road and bridge authority concerned where the gross weight of a loaded Special Types vehicle exceeds:

(a) 50,000kg
(b) 60,000kg
(c) 80,000kg
(d) 150,000kg

509. Special Types vehicles of category 1 carrying a load are restricted to a maximum speed on single carriageway roads of:

(a) 12mph
(b) 20mph
(c) 30mph
(d) 40mph

510. The maximum permitted weight for a category 3 Special Types vehicle and load is:

(a) 60 tonnes
(b) 76.2 tonnes
(c) 80 tonnes
(d) 150 tonnes

511. Under the Special Types General Order (STGO) a statutory attendant must be carried when the width of a vehicle or its load exceeds:

(a) 1.83 metres
(b) 2.5 metres
(c) 2.9 metres
(d) 3.5 metres

512. Under the Special Types General Order special authorisation from the Secretary of State for Transport is needed if the width of a vehicle and load exceeds:

(a) 3.5 metres
(b) 5.0 metres
(c) 6.0 metres
(d) 9.0 metres

513. Under the Special Types General Order an attendant must be carried when a vehicle and its load exceeds an overall length of:

(a) 15 metres
(b) 16.8 metres
(c) 18 metres
(d) 18.3 metres

514. A statutory attendant must accompany a vehicle travelling under the Special Types General Order when:

(a) the load projects 2 metres beyond the rear of the vehicle
(b) the vehicle and load are 4 metres wide
(c) the overall length of both vehicle and load is 15 metres
(d) a load projects to the front by 1.5 metres

515. When 5 abnormal indivisible loads normally requiring statutory attendants travel in convoy, attendants should be carried:

(a) on the first vehicle only
(b) on each alternate vehicle
(c) on the last vehicle only
(d) on the first and last vehicles in the convoy

516. Advance notice must be given to the police for each district when it is proposed to move a vehicle and load having a rearward projection exceeding:

(a) 3.05 metres
(b) 2.9 metres
(c) 1.83 metres
(d) 1.07 metres

517. A vehicle carrying a load which projects 1.50 metres beyond the front and 1.75 metres beyond the rear of the vehicle must be marked:

(a) so as to make the rear projection clearly visible
(b) with a front marker board only
(c) with a rear marker board only
(d) with both front and rear marker boards

518. Road vehicle C & U regulations require goods vehicles carrying rearward projecting loads exceeding 1.0 metre but not exceeding 2.0 metres to:

(a) have the projection made clearly visible
(b) display end and side marker boards
(c) display end and side marker boards and carry an attendant
(d) display end and side marker boards, carry an attendant and notify the police in advance

519. Marker boards used for indicating projecting loads must be:

(a) indirectly illuminated at night
(b) directly illuminated at night
(c) made of red fluorescent material on a white background
(d) made of red reflex reflecting material on a white background

520. Which of the following loads must be marked with side and end marker boards?

(a) a load projecting 2 metres rearward
(b) a load projecting 4 metres forward
(c) a load projecting 1.7 metres forward
(d) a load projecting 3 metres rearward

521. A vehicle with a load overhanging the rear by 1.9 metres requires:

(a) at least 2 clear days' advance notice to the police
(b) the projection to be made clearly visible
(c) the speed of the vehicle to be restricted to 30mph
(d) a statutory attendant to be carried on the vehicle

522. Where a load projects beyond the front of the vehicle by 3.09 metres the procedure should be to:

(a) notify the police 2 days in advance
(b) notify the police and carry a statutory attendant
(c) notify the police, carry a statutory attendant and display side and end marker boards
(d) notify the highway and bridge authorities

523. Regulations require that a goods vehicle carrying a rearward projecting load exceeding 2.0 metres but not exceeding 3.05 metres must have:

(a) an end marker board only
(b) both end and side marker boards
(c) both end and side marker boards and carry an attendant
(d) both end and side marker boards, carry an attendant, and advance notice must be given to the police

524. The load compartment of a vehicle which is designed to carry animals must be:

(a) suitably strengthened
(b) lined with insulating material
(c) lined with a washable surface
(d) free from sharp projections

525. Horses carried in road vehicles must be provided with food and water at intervals of at least:

(a) 4 hours
(b) 6 hours
(c) 10 hours
(d) 12 hours

526. Farm animals of different species may be carried in the same vehicle provided that they are separated by fixed partitions.

(a) True
(b) False

527. Records relating to the carriage of animals must be retained and be available for inspection for at least:

(a) 3 weeks
(b) 3 months
(c) 6 months
(d) 12 months

528. A food delivery driver who may need to carry meat carcasses must wear a hat so that the meat does not touch his hair.

(a) True
(b) False

B8 Vehicle Weights and Dimensions

529. The weight of a vehicle, inclusive of body and parts normally used in its operation but exclusive of the weight of water, fuel, loose tools and equipment and batteries used for propulsion, is defined as the:

(a) plated weight
(b) unladen weight
(c) tare weight
(d) kerbside weight

530. The total weight legally imposed on a road by a vehicle including driver, load, fuel, water and loose tools is the:

(a) kerbside weight
(b) payload
(c) unladen weight
(d) gross vehicle weight

531. The weight of a goods vehicle in road-going condition, inclusive of oil, water and fuel but without its load and without the driver, is defined as the:

(a) tare weight

(b) kerb weight
(c) unladen weight
(d) gross vehicle weight

532. When entering premises to collect bulk loads, vehicles usually cross a weighbridge to establish the weight of the empty vehicle complete with driver. This weight is called the:

(a) tare weight
(b) kerb weight
(c) maximum laden weight
(d) gross train weight

533. When calculating the maximum payload capacity for a rigid goods vehicle it is necessary to deduct:

(a) the kerb weight from the maximum laden weight
(b) the unladen weight from the gross train weight
(c) the tare weight from the permissible maximum weight
(d) the maximum laden weight from the gross vehicle weight

534. When determining the tare weight of a goods vehicle by weighing prior to loading, the weight should include:

(a) the driver, any passengers and a full tank of fuel
(b) any passengers to be carried and a full tank of fuel
(c) the driver only, passengers and fuel to be added later
(d) no driver or passengers and a low tank of fuel

535. The payload capacity of a vehicle can be obtained by deducting its kerbside weight from:

(a) the unladen weight
(b) the gross vehicle weight
(c) the total of axle weight
(d) the gross plated weight

536. In calculating the unladen weight of a vehicle which uses alternative bodies which of the following applies?

(a) the weight of the heaviest alternative bodies must be included
(b) the weight of the lightest of alternative bodies must be included
(c) the weight of the body most frequently used is included
(d) the weight of such bodies are not included

537. The maximum permitted weight at which a rigid goods vehicle may be used on roads in the UK is the:

(a) gross combination weight
(b) gross plated weight
(c) gross train weight
(d) kerbside weight

538. A 'motor car' is defined in law as a mechanically propelled vehicle constructed to carry goods or passengers and with an unladen weight not exceeding:

(a) 1,525kg
(b) 2,030kg
(o) 2,540kg
(d) 3,050kg

539. The term 'relevant axle spacing' used in connection with weight calculations for articulated vehicles means the distance between the:

(a) rear axle of the tractive unit and the rear axle of the semi-trailer
(b) rear axle of the tractive unit and the front axle of the semi-trailer
(c) front axle of the tractive unit and the front axle of the semi-trailer
(d) front axle of the tractive unit and the rear axle of the semi-trailer

540. A vehicle with a wheelbase of 6 metres is carrying a uniform load of 9,000kgs. If the centre line of the load is 3.0 metres from the front axle the weight on the rear axle will be:

(a) 4,500kg

(b) 5,000kg
(c) 5,600kg
(d) 5,800kg

541. A vehicle carrying a uniform load of 6 tonnes has a wheel base of 6 metres. If the distance from the centre of the load to the rear axle is 2 metres, the weight on the front axle will be:

(a) 2 tonnes
(b) 3 tonnes
(c) 5 tonnes
(d) 7 tonnes

542. The maximum weight for an axle fitted with two wheels transversely each equipped with twin tyres having centres not less than 300mm apart on a vehicle with a relevant train weight exceeding 32,520kg is:

(a) 9,200kg
(b) 10,170kg
(c) 10,500kg
(d) 11,000kg

543. The maximum weight which may be imposed on a single-wheel axle where there is no other wheel in line transversely is:

(a) 5,090kg
(b) 4,600kg
(c) 9,200kg
(d) 1,020kg

544. Where a vehicle is fitted with a bogie comprising 2 closely-spaced axles at least 1.85 metres apart and the plated weight of neither axle exceeds half the specified weight, the maximum weight for the bogie is:

(a) 18,800kg
(b) 19,320kg
(c) 20,000kg
(d) 20,340kg

545. For a vehicle/trailer fitted with 3 adjacent axles having a distance of at least 4.6 metres between the foremost

and rearmost axles, the maximum total weight permitted on the axles is:

(a) 18,290kg
(b) 20,330kg
(c) 22,360kg
(d) 24,390kg

546. If a tri-axle bogie on a semi-trailer is equipped with air suspension, the maximum weight permitted on each individual axle is:

(a) 6.0 tonnes
(b) 7.5 tonnes
(c) 8.0 tonnes
(d) 9.0 tonnes

547. When calculating the overall length of a vehicle which of the following items are excluded from the calculation?

(a) vehicle headlamps and fog lamps
(b) starting handle
(c) front-mounted towing eyes
(d) protective 'bump' stops on the rear of the body

548. The permitted maximum overall length for an articulated vehicle (not designed to carry indivisible loads of exceptional length) in the UK is:

(a) 11.5 metres
(b) 12 metres
(c) 15.5 metres
(d) 16.5 metres

549. The permitted maximum overall length for a road train in the UK comprising a rigid vehicle and draw-bar trailer is:

(a) 15 metres
(b) 16.5 metres
(c) 18 metres
(d) 18.5 metres

550. The maximum overall length for a vehicle and load permitted by the Special Types General Order is:

(a) 15.5 metres
(b) 16.5 metres
(c) 18.3 metres
(d) 27.4 metres

551. The maximum permitted length for a 2-axle rigid goods vehicle is:

(a) 11 metres
(b) 12 metres
(c) 15.5 metres
(d) 18 metres

552. The maximum permitted length for a pre-January 1990 semi-trailer used in international transport operations is:

(a) 12.2 metres
(b) 13.6 metres
(c) 16.5 metres
(d) not limited providing the combination does not exceed 15.5 metres

553. The maximum permitted length for a 3-axle rigid goods vehicle is:

(a) 11 metres
(b) 12 metres
(c) 13.6 metres
(d) 15 metres

554. Which of the following must be included when determining the overall width of a heavy goods vehicle?

(a) rear-view driving mirrors
(b) bodywork protection rubbing strakes
(c) a tailboard let down to facilitate loading
(d) a receptacle to contain a Customs seal

555. The maximum permitted width for a normal goods vehicle exceeding 3.5 tonnes is:

(a) 2 metres
(b) 2.3 metres

(c) 2.5 metres
(d) 2.75 metres

556. The maximum overall width for a vehicle defined as a 'heavy motor car' must not exceed:

(a) 2.1 metres
(b) 2.3 metres
(c) 2.5 metres
(d) 2.75 metres

557. The maximum permitted width of a trailer being drawn by a motor vehicle not exceeding 2 tonnes unladen weight is:

(a) 2.3 metres
(b) 2.5 metres
(c) 2.6 metres
(d) 2.75 metres

558. The legal height restriction of 4.2 metres on semi-trailers over 26,000kgs and forming part of an articulated combination running above 32,520kgs maximum laden weight:

(a) applies to a sheeted and roped load
(b) applies to any load restrained by flexible means
(c) does not apply to any detachable structure used to contain the load
(d) applies to any detachable structure used to contain the load

559. The maximum overhang permitted for rigid goods vehicles is:

(a) 50 per cent of the wheelbase
(b) 55 per cent of the wheelbase
(c) 60 per cent of the wheelbase
(d) 65 per cent of the wheelbase

560. The overhang of a 3-axled vehicle with a tandem rear bogie is measured from:

(a) the centre line between the rear axles
(b) a point 100mm behind the centre line between the rear axles

(c) a point 110mm behind the centre line between the rear axles
(d) a point 110mm ahead of the centre line between the rear axles

561. For the purposes of ensuring proper axle weight distribution, the removal of part of the load from the rear overhang of laden goods vehicle will:

(a) increase the load on both the front and rear axles
(b) reduce the load on both the front and rear axles
(c) decrease loading on the front axle and increase it on the rear axle
(d) increase loading on the front axle and decrease it on the rear axle

562. Regulations permit a maximum weight for a rigid goods vehicle having four or more axles of:

(a) 26,420kg
(b) 28,450kg
(c) 30,490kg
(d) 32,520kg

563. The total weight transmitted to the road surface by any two wheels in line transversely on an axle fitted with single tyres must not exceed:

(a) 9,000kg
(b) 9,100kg
(c) 9,200kg
(d) 9,500kg

564. A 5-axled articulated vehicle comprising a 2-axle tractive unit and tri-axle semi-trailer with a relevant axle spacing of at least 6.9 metres will have a maximum permissible weight of:

(a) 32,520kg
(b) 35,000kg
(c) 36,000kg
(d) 38,000kg

565. The maximum permitted weight for a 2-axled rigid goods vehicle is:

(a) 13,230kg
(b) 14,230kg
(c) 16,260kg
(d) 18,230kg

566. **An articulated vehicle with a single-axle semi-trailer and with a relevant axle spacing of 2.9 metres has a maximum permitted weight of:**

(a) 20,330kg
(b) 23,370kg
(c) 24,390kg
(d) 32,520kg

567. **In calculating the maximum permitted weight for an 8-wheel rigid goods vehicle it is necessary to know the distance between:**

(a) the two front steering axles
(b) the two axles of the rear bogie
(c) the rearmost front axle and the foremost rear axle
(d) the foremost axle and the rearmost axle

568. **As a general rule the wider the axle spacings on a goods vehicle the greater the maximum permissible weight.**

(a) True
(b) False

569. **The gross train weight shown on the DTp ('Ministry') plate attached to an articulated tractive unit is the total weight permitted in the UK for:**

(a) the tractive unit only
(b) the semi-trailer and load
(c) both the tractive unit and semi-trailer
(d) the load permitted to be carried on the vehicle

570. **If P = payload, W = wheelbase and D = distance from the centre line of the payload to the rear axle, then the load on the front axle is calculated by using the formula:**

(a) $\frac{P + D}{W}$

(b) $\frac{P \times D}{W}$
(c) $\frac{W \times D}{P}$
(d) $\frac{W \times P}{D}$

B9 Vehicle Selection

571. The gross plated weight of a rigid goods vehicle is:

(a) the maximum weight at which the vehicle is legally permitted to operate
(b) the total weight transmitted to the road by all the wheels of the laden vehicle
(c) the total weight of an unladen vehicle
(d) the total weight of a rigid vehicle and loaded draw-bar trailer

572. Which of the following is classed in law as a 'small goods vehicle'?

(a) a vehicle constructed to carry goods with a permissible maximum weight of 7 tonnes and drawing a trailer of 2 tonnes gross weight
(b) a vehicle constructed to carry goods with a permissible maximum weight of 3 tonnes and drawing a trailer of 1 tonne gross weight
(c) a vehicle constructed to carry goods with a permissible maximum weight of 2.5 tonnes and drawing a trailer of 1 tonne gross weight
(d) a vehicle constructed to carry goods with a permissible maximum weight of 3,550kg

573. A goods vehicle is legally defined as a 'motor car' if its unladen weight does not exceed:

(a) 2,500kg
(b) 2,750kg
(c) 3,050kg
(d) 3,500kg

574. A 'composite trailer' as defined in law is a combination of:

(a) a convertor dolly and an articulated semi-trailer
(b) a convertor dolly and a draw-bar trailer
(c) two semi-trailers joined together behind a rigid motor vehicle
(d) two draw-bar trailers joined together behind a motor vehicle

575. An articulated vehicle is defined in law as a heavy motor car with a trailer so attached that when the trailer is uniformly loaded a proportion of the weight of the load is transferred to the drawing vehicle amounting to:

(a) 10 per cent
(b) 15 per cent
(c) 20 per cent
(d) 25 per cent

576. The abbreviation GTW means:

(a) gross tare weight
(b) gross train weight
(c) gross trailer weight
(d) gross towing weight

577. The abbreviation GCW means:

(a) gross carrying weight
(b) gross combination weight
(c) gross chartered weight
(d) greater capacity weight

578. The term GTW applies to the gross weight of:

(a) a towing vehicle
(b) an articulated tractive unit
(c) a semi-trailer
(d) a vehicle and trailer combination

579. A 'medium sized goods vehicle' is defined in law as a vehicle constructed or adapted for the carriage of goods and which has a gross weight between:

(a) 2.5 tonnes and 5 tonnes
(b) 3 tonnes and 5 tonnes

(c) 3.5 tonnes and 7 tonnes
(d) 3.5 tonnes and 7.5 tonnes

580. A 'heavy motor car' is defined in law as a mechanically propelled vehicle not being a motor car which is constructed to carry a load or passengers and with an unladen weight which exceeds:

(a) 1,525kg
(b) 2,540kg
(c) 3,500kg
(d) 7,500kg

B10 Vehicle Plating and Testing

581. Application for heavy goods vehicle annual tests are made to:

(a) the local DTp goods vehicle testing station
(b) the Goods Vehicle Centre, Swansea
(c) the Licensing Authority for the traffic area in which the vehicle is kept
(d) the local Vehicle Registration Office

582. Heavy goods vehicle plating and annual testing applies to rigid goods vehicles exceeding:

(a) 1,020kg unladen weight
(b) 1,525kg unladen weight
(c) 1,750kg unladen weight
(d) 3,500kg gross weight

583. Under the regulations dealing with goods vehicle plating and annual testing, a part IV examination is:

(a) a test following a notifiable alteration to the vehicle
(b) re-examination of a vehicle following failure of a first test
(c) re-examination of a vehicle following failure of a periodical test
(d) re-examination of a vehicle following appeal against a test failure

584. To which of the following types of vehicle do the goods vehicle plating and annual testing regulations apply?

(a) articulated semi-trailers
(b) breakdown vehicles
(c) electrically-propelled motor vehicles
(d) engineering plant

585. Which of the following vehicles are exempt from goods vehicle plating and annual testing?

(a) vehicles first registered before 1 January 1961 and used unladen
(b) vehicles operated for the purposes of telecommunications
(c) refuse collection vehicles operated by a local authority
(d) electrically-propelled motor vehicles

586. The maximum gross weight at which a vehicle may be plated is reduced if it is fitted with tyres of a lower weight rating.

(a) True
(b) False

587. Under the goods vehicle plating and annual testing regulations, which of the following alterations must be notified to the Goods Vehicle Centre before the vehicle is used on the road?

(a) a change of registered keeper
(b) any change in the vehicle braking system
(c) a change of use
(d) a change of colour

588. The maximum gross weight at which a goods vehicle is plated is determined by:

(a) the vehicle manufacturer
(b) the Licensing Authority
(c) the Goods Vehicle Centre in conjunction with the manufacturer
(d) the Driver and Vehicle Licensing Centre, Swansea

589. A manufacturer's plate must be fitted to all goods vehicles (with certain exceptions) first used on or after 1 January 1968.

(a) True
(b) False

590. Where a vehicle displays both a manufacturer's plate and a DTp (ie 'Ministry') plate, the former takes precedence over the latter.

(a) True
(b) False

591. Which of the following items of information is not found on a 'Ministry' goods vehicle plate?

(a) the year of manufacture of the vehicle
(b) the maximum permissible weights not to be exceeded in GB
(c) the manufacturer's name and address
(d) the weights for all axles of the vehicle

592. A heavy goods vehicle testing station may refuse to test a vehicle or trailer for which of the following reasons?

(a) the driver did not produce a valid certificate of insurance
(b) the vehicle was in a dirty condition
(c) the vehicle was not accompanied by a competent motor fitter
(d) the trailer had been painted a different colour since the previous test

593. The Department of Transport may issue certificates of temporary exemption from goods vehicle annual testing requirements for a period not exceeding:

(a) 1 month
(b) 3 months
(c) 6 months
(d) 12 months

594. If a goods vehicle fails the annual test it may be re-submitted to the same test station for re-examination of the defective components only within:

(a) 1 week
(b) 8 days

(c) 14 days
(d) 3 weeks

595. Appeals against the results of a goods vehicle annual test should be made in the first instance to:

(a) the DTp Area Mechanical Engineer
(b) the DTp Goods Vehicle Test Station manager
(c) the Secretary of State for Transport
(d) the Goods Vehicle Centre, Swansea

596. Which of the following items need not be shown on a manufacturer's plate?

(a) the number of axles
(b) the vehicle type
(c) tyre ply ratings and maximum pressures
(d) maximum gross weight

597. Vehicles subject to goods vehicle annual testing must generally be submitted for their first annual test:

(a) by the third anniversary of the month of their original registration
(b) before the beginning of the first anniversary month of their original registration
(c) before the end of the first anniversary month of their original registration
(d) before the end of the first anniversary month of their date of manufacture

598. Following a first annual test of a goods vehicle, subsequent annual tests must be carried out:

(a) each year by the end of the anniversary month of the date of their first registration
(b) by the expiry date of the existing test certificate
(c) in the anniversary month of their date of original manufacture
(d) on a date allocated by the Goods Vehicle Centre, Swansea

599. Which of the following items need not be shown on the manufacturer's plate fitted to a goods carrying trailer?

(a) maximum gross weight
(b) year of original manufacture
(c) trailer chassis number
(d) place of manufacture

600. In exceptional circumstances, where it is not possible to have a vehicle tested by the due date, a temporary exemption certificate may be issued valid for:

(a) 3 months
(b) 6 months
(c) 12 months
(d) 15 months

601. Heavy goods vehicles subject to plating and annual testing become due for their first test:

(a) in the 6th month after original registration
(b) in the 11th month after original registration
(c) by the end of the 1st anniversary month of the date of first registration
(d) in the month following the anniversary of their first registration

602. One of the grounds on which a goods vehicle test station can refuse to test a vehicle is:

(a) if it is in a dirty condition
(b) if the driver is not accompanied by a skilled fitter
(c) if it is laden
(d) if an articulated vehicle arrives with a semi-trailer attached

603. Which of the following is not a notifiable alteration under goods vehicle plating and annual testing?

(a) fitting an extra axle to increase the vehicle carrying capacity
(b) an alteration which increases the rear overhang by more than 1 foot
(c) fitting a body of a different construction
(d) fitting tyres of a different make

604. Where a goods vehicle operator carries out a notifiable alteration on his vehicle he must:

(a) advise the Goods Vehicle Centre, Swansea
(b) send the vehicle registration document to Swansea for amendment
(c) apply for a new plate and plating certificate
(d) obtain a new Type Approval certificate

605. In accordance with the Freight Containers (Safety Convention) Regulations 1984, safety approval plates for freight containers are issued by:

(a) the Road Haulage Association
(b) Department of Transport goods vehicle test stations
(c) a body appointed by the Health and Safety Executive
(d) Lloyds Register of Shipping

B11 Construction and Use Regulations

606. A Certificate of Conformity relating to a vehicle indicates that it conforms to:

(a) Type Approval standards
(b) a specified British Standard
(c) a BS Quality Standard
(d) goods vehicle plating requirements

607. Since the introduction of Type Approval, goods vehicles subject to plating and annual testing are issued with a DTp plate:

(a) at the point of manufacture
(b) when first presented for annual test
(c) when first specified on a goods vehicle 'O' licence
(d) when first registered

608. Which of the following items is covered by the goods vehicle Type Approval regulations?

(a) exhaust emissions
(b) the aim of vehicle headlights
(c) the strength of rear bumpers
(d) the ply rating for tyres

609. National Type Approval for goods vehicles is also applicable to:

(a) locomotives
(b) motor tractors
(c) breakdown vehicles
(d) 4-wheel-drive dual-purpose vehicles

610. If the fuel tank supplying petrol for an engine used to drive ancillary equipment on a vehicle is made of plastic:

(a) there is no contravention of the law
(b) the law is contravened because the fuel should be supplied from the main tank
(c) the law is contravened because the fuel tank should be made of metal to conform to C & U regulations requirements
(d) the law is contravened because ancillary equipment should only be driven by diesel fuel

611. Excess fuel devices fitted to diesel-engined vehicles must not be used when the vehicle is in motion.

(a) True
(b) False

612. Which of the following items are not covered by the road vehicles Construction and Use regulations?

(a) windscreen washers and wipers
(b) rear-view mirrors
(c) vehicle registration plates
(d) windscreen glass

613. It is an offence to sound the horn of a motor vehicle on a restricted road between:

(a) 22.30 hours and 07.30 hours
(b) 23.30 hours and 07.30 hours
(c) 23.00 hours and 07.00 hours
(d) 23.30 hours and 07.00 hours

614. The law requiring a road vehicle to have an audible warning device does not apply to:

(a) a moped
(b) vehicles used under a trade licence

(c) military vehicles
(d) a vehicle not capable of exceeding 20mph on the level

615. Gongs, bells and two-tone horns are not permitted on:

(a) vehicles used by the police
(b) military vehicles used for bomb-disposal purposes
(c) breakdown vehicles used for emergency recovery work
(d) vehicles used by the Blood Transfusion Service

616. Goods vehicles must be fitted with:

(a) three mirrors, two fitted externally and one internally
(b) two mirrors fitted externally on the offside and on the nearside
(c) two mirrors, one fitted internally and one externally on the nearside
(d) two mirrors, one externally on the offside and the other fitted either internally or externally on the nearside

617. Where two rear-view mirrors are required on goods vehicles to comply with the law they must show traffic:

(a) to the rear only
(b) to the rear and nearside rearwards
(c) to the rear and offside rearwards
(d) to the rear and both sides rearwards

618. Seat belts must be fitted to which of the following vehicles?

(a) taxis and private hire vehicles
(b) vehicles being driven on a road test under a trade licence
(c) a light van first registered since 1 April 1967
(d) a goods vehicle with a maximum gross weight of 3,550kg

619. When a broken-down vehicle is being towed by means of a rope or chain, the maximum distance permitted between the two vehicles is:

(a) 1.5 metres
(b) 4 metres
(c) 4.5 metres
(d) 5 metres

620. Spray suppression devices must be fitted to all trailers built since 1 May 1985 and which have a maximum gross weight exceeding:

(a) 3.5 tonnes
(b) 7.5 tonnes
(c) 10 tonnes
(d) 16 tonnes

621. Spray suppression devices must be fitted to all new goods vehicles first used since 1 April 1986 and exceeding:

(a) 7.5 tonnes gross weight
(b) 10 tonnes gross weight
(c) 12 tonnes gross weight
(d) 16 tonnes gross weight

622. Sideguards are legally required on new goods vehicles exceeding 3,500kg maximum gross weight if the distance between any two consecutive axles exceeds:

(a) 2.0 metres
(b) 2.5 metres
(c) 3.0 metres
(d) 3.5 metres

623. Rear underrun protection is required on most new rigid goods vehicles where the maximum gross weight exceeds:

(a) 1,020kg
(b) 1,525kg
(c) 2,040kg
(d) 3,500kg

624. Rear underrun protection is not required on goods vehicles incapable of exceeding a maximum speed on a level road of:

(a) 10mph
(b) 15mph
(c) 20mph
(d) 25mph

625. Rear underrun protection is required on goods-carrying trailers manufactured on or after 1 May 1983 and with an unladen weight exceeding:

(a) 1,020kg
(b) 2,040kg
(c) 3,500kg
(d) 750kg

626. The maximum noise level permitted for a light goods vehicle 'in use' is:

(a) 81 decibels
(b) 84 decibels
(c) 87 decibels
(d) 92 decibels

627. Regulations require vehicles to be equipped with safety glass in:

(a) the windscreen only
(b) the windscreen and windows to the front
(c) the windscreen, windows to the front and those on the offside of the driver's seat
(d) the windscreen, windows to the front and those on either side of the driver's seat

628. The vehicle Construction and Use regulations require every vehicle having a fixed windscreen to be fitted with:

(a) one efficient automatic windscreen wiper
(b) one or more efficient automatic windscreen wipers
(c) at least two efficient automatic windscreen wipers
(d) an adequate method of clearing the windscreen

629. A driver who stopped at a motorway service station found when he returned to his vehicle that vandals had damaged his windscreen wipers. The law:

(a) requires him to leave the motorway at the next available exit
(b) requires him to notify the police before proceeding to the nearest garage for repairs
(c) allows him complete his journey before having the wipers repaired
(d) prohibits him from taking the vehicle on the public highway until the wipers are repaired and function efficiently

630. It is not an offence to drive a motor vehicle without efficient windscreen wipers:

(a) when it is not raining
(b) if the vehicle is not capable of travelling at more than 30mph
(c) if the driver can obtain an adequate view to the front without looking through the windscreen
(d) if the vehicle was first registered before 1 January 1940

631. Legal requirements regarding the fitment of pneumatic tyres on motor vehicles do not apply to:

(a) vehicles incapable of travelling at more than 20mph
(b) vehicles operated under a trade licence
(c) vehicles being towed to a scrapyard to be broken up
(d) vehicles used mainly for work on rough ground

632. Regulations currently specify a minimum depth for the tread on motor vehicle tyres of:

(a) 1mm
(b) 1.5mm
(c) 1.6mm
(d) 2.1mm

633. The minimum tread depth specified in law for tyres fitted to motor vehicles and trailers must extend to:

(a) the whole breadth and around three-quarters of the circumference

(b) three-quarters of the breadth and around the entire circumference
(c) the whole breadth and around the entire circumference
(d) half the breadth and around the entire circumference

634. A 'wide tyre' as defined in regulations is one having a minimum width in contact with the road surface of:

(a) 200mm
(b) 250mm
(c) 300mm
(d) 350mm

635. Regulations state that a pneumatic tyre fitted to a motor vehicle must not have a cut deep enough to reach the ply or cord in excess of:

(a) 10 per cent of the section width
(b) 25mm or 10 per cent of the section width
(c) 25mm or 15 per cent of the section width
(d) 25mm or 20 per cent of the section width

636. Re-cut tyres may be used on vehicles legally defined as 'motor cars' providing the wheel rim diameter exceeds:

(a) 300mm
(b) 305mm
(c) 400mm
(d) 405mm

637. Motor vehicles first used since 1 January 1968 must have a service brake with a minimum efficiency of:

(a) 45 per cent
(b) 50 per cent
(c) 55 per cent
(d) 60 per cent

638. In the event of failure of one part of a split braking system on a vehicle, the remaining part of the system must have an efficiency of not less than:

(a) 25 per cent

(b) 30 per cent
(c) 40 per cent
(d) 45 per cent

639. The minimum specified braking efficiencies for pre-1968 motor vehicles drawing a trailer are:

(a) service brake 35 per cent and secondary brake 15 per cent
(b) service brake 45 per cent and secondary brake 20 per cent
(c) service brake 45 per cent and secondary brake 25 per cent
(d) service brake 50 per cent and secondary brake 25 per cent

640. A new vehicle with a maximum permissible weight of 16 tonnes has a service braking system with an efficiency of 45 per cent and a secondary system with an efficiency of 25 per cent. Legal requirements are met by:

(a) both braking systems
(b) the service braking system only
(c) the secondary braking system only
(d) neither braking system

641. The law requires new goods vehicles to have a parking brake capable of holding the vehicle (without the assistance of stored energy) on a gradient of at least:

(a) 12 per cent
(b) 16 per cent
(c) 25 per cent
(d) 50 per cent

642. The parking brake of new motor cars and heavy motor cars must be capable of holding the vehicle and any trailer attached on a maximum gradient of:

(a) 10 per cent
(b) 12 per cent
(c) 16 per cent
(d) 25 per cent

643. Which of the following vehicle and trailer combinations may legally be used on a public road?

(a) a rigid goods vehicle drawing 2 unladen trailers
(b) a rigid goods vehicle drawing 1 laden and 1 unladen trailer
(c) a rigid goods vehicle drawing 1 laden trailer
(d) a motor tractor drawing 2 laden trailers

644. When a broken-down vehicle has to be towed, the law requires:

(a) the towing vehicle to display an amber flashing beacon
(b) the towed vehicle to display the words 'on tow' at the rear
(c) the towing vehicle to travel with its headlamps illuminated
(d) the registration mark of the towing vehicle to be displayed on the rear of the towed vehicle

645. A vehicle defined in law as a locomotive may draw 2 laden trailers.

(a) True
(b) False

646. A towing vehicle with an permissible maximum weight not exceeding 3,500kg is permitted to tow a trailer with a maximum length of:

(a) 5 metres
(b) 7 metres
(c) 11 metres
(d) 12 metres

B12 Vehicle Lighting and Marking

647. Lighting regulations require which of the following lamps to be fitted to all goods vehicles?

(a) 2 front-mounted spot or fog lamps
(b) 2 rear fog lamps
(c) 1 rear number plate lamp

(d) 1 or 2 reversing lamps

648. When driving a vehicle during daylight hours which has a defective front position lamp the legal situation is that:

(a) the driver will not be convicted of an offence if he can prove that the light became defective during the journey in progress
(b) no offence is committed if the other vehicle lights remain operational
(c) an offence is committed because all vehicle lights must be in good working order at all times
(d) an offence will only be committed if the vehicle is driven during the hours of darkness

649. Under current vehicle lighting regulations, vehicle lights must be used:

(a) from sunset to sunrise
(b) from half an hour after sunset to half an hour after sunrise
(c) from half an hour before sunset to half an hour before sunrise
(d) from an hour after sunset to an hour before sunrise

650. With certain exceptions, goods vehicles first used on or after 1 April 1980 must be fitted with at least:

(a) 1 rear fog lamp
(b) 2 rear fog lamps
(c) 1 front-mounted spot lamp
(d) 2 front-mounted fog lamps

651. Two rear red stop lamps are required on all motor vehicles first used since:

(a) 1 January 1970
(b) 1 December 1970
(c) 1 January 1971
(d) 1 December 1971

652. Vehicle lighting regulations require obligatory dipped-beam headlamps to be fitted at at maximum distance from the side of the vehicle of:

(a) 400mm
(b) 500mm
(c) 600mm
(d) 700mm

653. Regulations require that obligatory headlamps on new vehicles must be fitted not less and not more than specified distances from the ground of?

(a) 300mm and 600mm
(b) 400mm and 800mm
(c) 500mm and 1000mm
(d) 500mm and 1200mm

654. Dipped beam headlamps must be fitted to all vehicles capable of travelling at a speed in excess of:

(a) 5mph
(b) 10mph
(c) 15mph
(d) 20mph

655. Obligatory headlamps must be used during the hours of darkness in any unlit area where the street lamps are positioned more than:

(a) 150 yards apart
(b) 200 yards apart
(c) 225 yards apart
(d) 250 yards apart

656. A matching pair of correctly mounted front fog lamps may be used in place of dipped headlamps:

(a) not at all
(b) in severely reduced visibility at any time
(c) in severely reduced visibility during the hours of darkness
(d) only in conditions of fog or falling snow

657. Where front position lamps are required by law to be fitted to trailers drawn by motor vehicles they must be positioned:

(a) a maximum distance of 150mm from the side

(b) a minimum distance of 300mm from the side
(c) a minimum distance of 450mm from the side
(d) a maximum distance of 450mm from the side

658. Side marker lamps must be carried on each side of the vehicle or load where the total length of the vehicle or combination of vehicles exceeds:

(a) 13 metres
(b) 15 metres
(c) 18.3 metres
(d) 20.3 metres

659. The 1989 vehicle lighting regulations require side marker lamps to be fitted to trailers with an overall length exceeding:

(a) 8.15 metres
(b) 9.15 metres
(c) 9.45 metres
(d) 10 metres

660. Side marker lamps are required when 2 vehicles in combination (other than an articulated vehicle) are carrying a supported load where the overall length inclusive of the load:

(a) is between 12.2 metres and 18.3 metres
(b) exceeds 18.3 metres
(c) does not exceed 12.2 metres
(d) exceeds 25.9 metres

661. The maximum wattage permitted by regulations for a reversing lamp not bearing an approval mark is:

(a) 7 watts
(b) 21 watts
(c) 24 watts
(d) 30 watts

662. Vehicle lighting regulations limit the wattage of stop lamps (other than those bearing an approval mark) fitted to post-1971 registered vehicles to:

(a) 5 to 15 watts

(b) 10 to 25 watts
(c) 15 to 36 watts
(d) a minimum of 36 watts

663. The law requires fitment of amber side-facing retro reflectors to normal rigid goods vehicles first registered since 1 April 1986 and exceeding a length of:

(a) 6 metres
(b) 8 metres
(c) 9 metres
(d) 11 metres

664. Two amber side-facing retro reflectors must be fitted on each side of trailers longer than:

(a) 4.5 metres
(b) 5 metres
(c) 6 metres
(d) 9 metres

665. Regulations limit the minimum and maximum height above the ground for the fitment of amber side-facing retro reflectors on vehicles to between:

(a) 400mm and 1,000mm
(b) 500mm and 1,200mm
(c) 600mm and 1,500mm
(d) 350mm and 1,500mm

666. Which of the following vehicles must legally display amber light from a rotating beacon?

(a) private ambulances
(b) breakdown vehicles attending a roadside breakdown
(c) breakdown vehicles while towing a disabled vehicle
(d) vehicles not capable of exceeding 25mph

667. The rate at which direction indicator lamps must flash is between:

(a) 50 and 100 times per minute

(b) 60 and 100 times per minute
(c) 60 and 120 times per minute
(d) 60 and 130 times per minute

668. To meet the legal requirements for direction indicators, vehicles first used since 1 April 1986 must be fitted with:

(a) 1 side indicator on each side
(b) 1 shoulder indicator and 1 rear indicator on each side
(c) 1 front and 1 rear indicator on each side
(d) 1 front, 1 rear and 1 side repeater indicator on each side

669. Rear reflective markings of red fluorescent and yellow reflective material must be fitted to rigid goods vehicles first registered after 1 August 1982 which exceed:

(a) 3,500kg maximum gross weight
(b) 6,000kg maximum gross weight
(c) 7,500kg maximum gross weight
(d) 8,000kg maximum gross weight

670. Which of the following classes of vehicle is exempt from the need to be fitted with rear reflective markers?

(a) goods vehicles over 7.5 tonnes gross
(b) trailers over 3.5 tonnes gross
(c) vehicles operating on trade plates
(d) articulated tractive units

671. Diagonal rear reflective markers may be fitted to which of the following vehicles or trailers?

(a) rigid vehicles more than 13 metres long
(b) trailers in combination more than 13 metres long
(c) rigid vehicles not more than 13 metres long
(d) trailers in combination more than 16.5 metres long

672. Red and yellow rear reflective marker displaying the words 'LONG VEHICLE' must be displayed at the rear of a trailer in combination exceeding:

(a) 11 metres
(b) 12 metres
(c) 13 metres
(d) 15 metres

673. When positioning lights on rearward projecting loads the light must be fitted a specified distance measured from:

(a) the rearmost point of the vehicle
(b) the existing vehicle rear lamps
(c) the existing vehicle rear reflectors
(d) the rearmost projection of the load

674. A vehicle which carries a load projecting 450mm beyond each side must display between sunset and sunrise:

(a) normal front and rear position lights
(b) additional front and rear position lamps fitted not more than 400mm from the extreme edges of each side of the load
(c) additional front and rear position lamps fitted anywhere on the load
(d) additional red position lights to the rear

B13 Fleet Inspection and Roadside Checks

675. Which of the following officials are authorised to issue vehicle prohibition and defect notices?

(a) an officer of HM Customs and Excise
(b) a Trading Standards officer
(c) a DTp traffic examiner
(d) a Department of Transport vehicle examiner

676. If a police officer in uniform stops a vehicle and issues the driver with a GV3 notice this is a direction:

(a) to drive the vehicle to a place where it can be examined
(b) to reduce the vehicle weight to within legal limits
(c) to produce his driving licence at a police station within 7 days

(d) preventing the vehicle being driven until it has been inspected

677. An immediate prohibition notice issued by a Department of Transport authorised vehicle examiner applies:

(a) to the use of the vehicle for any purpose
(b) to the use of the vehicle for specific purposes
(c) to the use of the vehicle above a specified maximum speed
(d) so as to prevent the carriage of goods on the vehicle

678. When a vehicle is found to have a defect that would not render it a danger to other road users, an authorised vehicle examiner would issue form:

(a) PG9
(b) PG9B
(c) PG10
(d) GV219

679. The official notice used by Department of Transport vehicle examiners to direct a vehicle to be taken to a specific place (not more than 5 miles away) for examination is form:

(a) GV3
(b) GV219
(c) PG9B
(d) GV160

680. A PG9 vehicle prohibition notice can be delayed before it takes effect up to a maximum of:

(a) 5 days
(b) 7 days
(c) 10 days
(d) 14 days

681. A haulier with no facilities of his own contracts with a local garage for the inspection and repair of his vehicles. If one of his vehicles on the road is subsequently found to have defects:

(a) the LA will hold the haulier responsible for the defects
(b) the LA will hold the garage responsible for the defects
(c) both the garage and the haulier are liable to be prosecuted
(d) the haulier can escape liability as he has a contract with the garage

682. A vehicle operator has an immediate right of appeal against the imposition of a prohibition notice by a DTp vehicle examiner at a roadside check.

(a) True
(b) False

683. If a DTp vehicle examiner refuses to remove a PG9 vehicle prohibition notice, the operator may appeal to:

(a) the Road Haulage Association
(b) the DTp Area Mechanical Engineer
(c) the Licensing Authority
(d) a goods vehicle test station manager

684. When a PG9 immediate prohibition is issued for a vehicle defect, a form PG9B will usually also be issued to:

(a) remove the prohibition
(b) allow the vehicle to move under certain conditions
(c) refuse permission for the the vehicle to be removed
(d) notify the operator to reduce the weight of the load

685. Following the imposition of a PG9 prohibition on a vehicle, repairs are carried out and it is presented for clearance. If the goods vehicle examiner imposes a GV9C this means:

(a) the prohibition has been removed
(b) the vehicle is still not roadworthy and the original prohibition remains in force
(c) the vehicle can be driven away subject to certain conditions
(d) only minor attention is still needed so the vehicle can be used

686. A goods vehicle subject to a PG9 prohibition by a DTp vehicle examiner is re-submitted to a test station where form PG10 is issued. This means:

(a) the examiner refuses to remove the prohibition
(b) the defects are cleared and the prohibition has been removed
(c) further defects are found and the prohibition remains in force
(d) further defects are found and another prohibition is applied

687. A PG9 prohibition notice imposed on a goods vehicle can only be completely removed by the issue of form:

(a) PG9A
(b) PG9B
(c) PG9C
(d) PG10

688. Issue of a form GV219 defect notice means:

(a) that the vehicle has been inspected by a DTp vehicle examiner
(b) that the operator is to be prosecuted for maintenance offences
(c) confirmation that a prohibition notice has been issued
(d) the vehicle has defects which, in the interest of road safety, should be rectified

689. When a goods vehicle has been weighed at a roadside check and found to be within legal limits, a certificate of weight is issued exempting the vehicle from further weight checks

(a) within the next 7 days
(b) at DTp weigh-stations during the next 24 hours
(c) during the continuance of the same journey with the same load
(d) before the vehicle returns to its authorised operating centre

690. If a goods vehicle is found at a DTp roadside check to be loaded in excess of legal limits, the driver will be issued with a prohibition notice on form:

(a) PG9
(b) PG10
(c) GV160
(d) GV219

691. When an authorised examiner is refused permission to carry out vehicle inspections on an operator's premises he can exercise his powers to enter the premises for the purpose, provided he gives notice in writing:

(a) at least 24 hours in advance
(b) at least 36 hours in advance
(c) at least 48 hours in advance
(d) sent by recorded delivery at least 72 hours in advance

692. A police constable in uniform can instruct the driver of a stationary goods vehicle to take it to a place for inspection (without risk of claims) not more than:

(a) 3 miles away
(b) 5 miles away
(c) 7 miles away
(d) 10 miles away

693. An authorised vehicle examiner can legally divert a vehicle to a place for weighing or inspection (without risk of claims) for a distance not exceeding:

(a) 1 mile
(b) 2 miles
(c) 5 miles
(d) 7 miles

694. When a vehicle has been diverted by an authorised examiner to a weighbridge more than 5 miles distant and the weight is found to be within legal limits:

(a) the operator has no claim for the delay to the journey
(b) the operator can claim a standard mileage allowance from the DTp
(c) a claim for expenses can be made to the highway authority

(d) an appeal can be made to the Secretary of State for Transport

B14 Operators' Licensing

695. Operators' licensing in Great Britain is based on the concept of quality control of road transport.

(a) True
(b) False

696. Implementation in the UK of EC Directive 561/74 resulted in a change to the pre-existing 'O' licensing scheme by requiring:

(a) certain transport managers to be professionally competent
(b) goods vehicle operators to specify suitable parking facilities
(c) the mandatory introduction of tachographs
(d) own-account transport operators to hold 'O' licences

697. The Road Traffic Act 1974 added further conditions to 'O' licensing requirements by demanding that licence holders:

(a) specify a suitable operating centre at which to base their vehicles
(b) must advertise licence applications in local newspapers
(c) specify the name of a professionally competent person
(d) retain vehicle maintenance records for 15 months

698. In connection with operators' licensing a 'small goods vehicle' is defined as a rigid vehicle with a permissible maximum weight not exceeding:

(a) 1,525kg
(b) 1,750kg
(c) 2,040kg
(d) 3,500kg

699. Which of the following vehicles is exempt from 'O' licensing?

(a) a vehicle constructed to carry goods with a permissible maximum weight of 3 tonnes and drawing a trailer of 2 tonnes gross weight
(b) a vehicle constructed to carry goods with a permissible maximum weight of 2 tonnes and drawing a trailer of 1,050kg unladen
(c) a vehicle constructed to carry goods with a permissible maximum weight of 3.5 tonnes drawing a trailer of 1.5 tonnes gross weight
(d) a vehicle constructed to carry goods with a permissible maximum weight of 7.4 tonnes

700. A goods vehicle standard 'O' licence is required by the user of a goods vehicle which is:

(a) over 3.5 tonnes gross weight in connection with hire or reward haulage
(b) carrying only the user's 'own goods'
(c) over 3.5 tonnes for carrying horses for leisure purposes
(d) used unladen solely for training purposes

701. A basic legal requirement for the grant of an 'O' licence is that the applicant must:

(a) guarantee to provide services at lower rates than existing hauliers
(b) comply with the law on drivers' hours and record keeping
(c) prove need for his services which is not met by other local operators
(d) not run services which compete with other modes of transport

702. A person wishing to enter the road haulage industry will require a standard national 'O' licence to operate:

(a) a rigid vehicle of 5 tonnes unladen weight
(b) a rigid vehicle of 3 tonnes gross plated weight
(c) an articulated vehicle of 3.5 tonnes gross train weight
(d) a dual-purpose vehicle and trailer

703. A restricted 'O' licence confines the holder to:

- (a) operations within a radius of 50km from the operating centre
- (b) operations within a radius of 75km from the Traffic Area office
- (c) undertake hire or reward haulage operations only
- (d) own-account transport operations

704. A manufacturer who plans to operate heavy goods vehicles for distribution of his own goods and occasional loads for customers for hire or reward in the UK and across Europe requires what type of 'O' licence?

- (a) a standard national licence
- (b) a restricted licence
- (c) a restricted international licence
- (d) a standard national and international licence

705. A road haulier applying for an 'O' licence must make:

- (a) separate applications to each Traffic Area in which he has an operating centre
- (b) a consolidated application to the DTp at Marsham Street, London
- (c) a single application to only one Traffic Area irrespective of how many operating centres he has
- (d) a single consolidated application to the Transport Tribunal

706. The maximum period for which an operator's licence will be issued in the UK is normally:

- (a) 2 years
- (b) 3 years
- (c) 4 years
- (d) 5 years

707. A company holding a restricted operator's licence is permitted to:

- (a) collect and deliver its own goods within the UK and on the continent
- (b) collect and deliver its own goods and goods for hire or reward within the UK and on the continent

(c) collect and deliver goods for hire or reward or own account but only in the UK
(d) collect and deliver its own goods in the UK only

708. When a company applies for a restricted operator's licence the Licensing Authority will not expect the applicant to:

(a) arrange to observe the drivers' hours and records regulations
(b) nominate the name of a person who is professionally qualified
(c) show he has adequate financial resources
(d) show that he is a fit and proper person to hold a licence

709. Provided an operator has a current goods vehicle 'O' licence he can operate as many vehicles as he wishes.

(a) True
(b) False

710. If an operator has 2 operating centres in one Traffic Area and 1 operating centre in another he must hold:

(a) 1 operator's licence to cover all the centres
(b) 2 operator's licences in 1 Traffic Area
(c) 3 separate operator's licences, 1 for each centre
(d) 2 operator's licences, 1 in each Traffic Area

711. Windscreen discs issued to a restricted 'O' licence holder are coloured:

(a) green
(b) orange
(c) blue
(d) yellow

712. In determining the previous conduct of an applicant for an 'O' licence , the LA will require a declaration of any convictions incurred during the past:

(a) 3 years
(b) 5 years
(c) 7 years

(d) 10 years

713. When completing the statement of intent on form GV79, the applicant for an 'O' licence is not required to declare that:

(a) the wages he pays his drivers will comply with Wages Council rates
(b) he will arrange to ensure that drivers comply with the hours and tachograph law
(c) vehicle maintenance arrangements will be adequate
(d) vehicles will not be overloaded

714. The maximum number of 'O' licences that an operator can hold in any one Traffic Area is:

(a) 1
(b) 2
(c) 3
(d) 4

715. The professional competence qualification for goods vehicle 'O' licensing can be met:

(a) collectively by a partnership
(b) only by an individual person
(c) by a private limited company
(d) by the board of directors of a public limited company

716. Full membership of a list of specified professional bodies is one means of meeting the qualification for professional competence but not including:

(a) the Chartered Institute of Transport (CIT)
(a) the Institute of Road Transport Engineers (IRTE)
(c) the Institute of Transport Administration (IoTA)
(d) the Institute of Logistics and Distribution Management

717. When a specified employee transport manager who meets the professional competence qualification ceases to be of good repute, the 'O' licence will:

(a) immediately become invalid
(b) continue in force for 6 months to allow for the appointment of a replacement professionally qualified person
(c) continue in force for 12 months to allow for the appointment of a replacement professionally qualified person
(d) continue in force for a 'reasonable period of time' to allow for the appointment of a replacement professionally qualified person

718. If a self-employed standard 'O' licence holder dies or becomes legally incapacitated, the LA can defer revocation of the licence on the takeover of the business if the new owner gives notice of the death to the LA within:

(a) 24 hours
(b) 2 weeks
(c) 2 months
(d) 6 months

719. If 12 months after the death of the designated transport manager an 'O' licence holder has not employed a qualified replacement and as a result the LA takes his licence away, this is defined as:

(a) a suspension of the licence
(b) a refusal to grant the licence
(c) a revocation of the licence
(d) a curtailment of the licence

720. Under the Goods Vehicles (Operators Licensing, Qualifications and Fees) Regulations 1984, as amended, the term 'financial standing' means:

(a) the value of the vehicles to be specified on the 'O' licence
(b) the authorised share capital of the transport business
(c) the average profitability of the business in previous years
(d) the availability of sufficient funds to ensure the legal operation of the transport undertaking

721. **Legal requirements for standards of 'good repute' in connection with an application for and the holding of an 'O' licence apply to:**

- **(a) the licence applicant/holder only**
- **(b) the operator and all his employees**
- **(c) both the applicant and the named professionally competent person**
- **(d) only the nominated professionally competent transport manager**

722. **'O' licence holders must advise the LA of any event which affects their good repute, professional competence or financial standing within a period of:**

- **(a) 7 days**
- **(b) 14 days**
- **(c) 28 days**
- **(d) 2 months**

723. **The law relating to operator's licensing requires that records of vehicle maintenance must be retained for at least:**

- **(a) 3 months**
- **(b) 6 months**
- **(c) 12 months**
- **(d) 15 months**

724. **If an 'O' licence vehicle windscreen disc is lost the licence holder must:**

- **(a) apply to the Traffic Area for a replacement on form GV79**
- **(b) apply to the Traffic Area for a replacement on form GV80**
- **(c) apply to the Traffic Area for a replacement on form GV81**
- **(d) notify the LA of the loss and a free replacement will be issued**

725. **When an operator needs to vary his 'O' licence his application should be sent to the LA at least:**

- **(a) 3 weeks in advance**

(b) 4 weeks in advance
(c) 6 weeks in advance
(d) 9 weeks in advance

726. The LA must be informed of any changes concerning the legal entity of an 'O' licence holder's business within:

(a) 7 days
(b) 14 days
(c) 28 days
(d) 2 months

727. For the purposes of goods vehicle 'O' licensing an 'operating centre' is defined as:

(a) the place where vehicles are inspected, serviced and repaired
(b) the licence holder's place of business where vehicle records are kept
(c) the place where vehicles are kept when not in use
(d) the registered office of the licence holder's business

728. If an operator parks his vehicles at the premises of a major customer, has them maintained at a commercial garage, and runs the business from his home, officially the 'operating centre' specified on his 'O' licence will be:

(a) his home
(b) the driver's home
(c) the repair garage
(d) the customer's premises

729. Which of the following bodies has a statutory right to object to the grant of a goods vehicle operators' licence?

(a) the Road Transport Industry Training Board
(b) the Health and Safety Executive
(c) the Road Haulage Association
(d) the Department of Transport

730. Which of the following organisations can legally object to an application for a goods vehicle 'O' licence?

(a) the National Association of Warehouse Keepers (NAWK)
(b) the British Institute of Forwarding Agents (BIFA)
(c) the British Association of Removers (BAR)
(d) the Royal Automobile Club (RAC)

731. Which of the following is one of the grounds for a trade union to make a statutory objection to the grant of an operators' licence?

(a) if the applicant has insufficient funds to maintain vehicles
(b) if there is a surplus of unemployed haulage drivers in that area
(c) if the applicant has not set up satisfactory health and safety schemes
(d) if the applicant refuses to recognise a closed shop agreement

732. Under 'O' licensing regulations an advertisement must be placed in a newspaper circulating in the locality of the proposed operating centre within a period:

(a) not exceeding 21 days before the application is made
(b) from 21 days before to 21 days after the application is made
(c) no later than 21 days after the application is made
(d) of any 42 days before or after the application

733. A person wishing to make an environmental representation against an 'O' licence application following publication of details in a newspaper must send this to the LA within:

(a) 10 days
(b) 21 days
(c) 28 days
(d) 30 days

734. When a statutory objection is made to an application for a goods vehicle 'O' licence the objector must send a copy of his letter to:

(a) the Chief Constable of police
(b) other statutory objectors
(c) the local authority
(d) the applicant at his published address

735. Apart from the list of statutory objectors, which of the following can make an environmental representation against the grant of an 'O' licence?

(a) the National Union of Railwaymen
(b) the local planning authority
(c) the Health and Safety Executive
(d) occupants of a neighbouring block of flats

736. Certain trades unions have a statutory right of objection to the grant of 'O' licences on the grounds that applicants:

(a) have poor industrial relations records
(b) have not set up proper safe-working arrangements
(c) have refused to be party to collective bargaining agreements
(d) are not persons of good repute

737. An 'O' licence holder who acquires additional vehicles within the number currently authorised on his licence:

(a) should have notified the LA before he acquired them
(b) must notify the LA within 1 month of acquiring them using form GV80
(c) must notify the LA within 3 months using form GV80
(d) has no legal need to inform the LA

738. A licence holder who wishes to expand his fleet beyond the total number of vehicles currently authorised on his 'O' licence must:

(a) apply for an additional licence to cover the extra vehicles
(b) make a GV81 application to vary his licence
(c) surrender his existing licence and apply for a new one

(d) defer the expansion until his current licence expires

739. An operator may transfer a vehicle from one Traffic Area to another in which he holds an 'O' licence without informing the LA, for a period of up to:

(a) 1 month
(b) 2 months
(c) 3 months
(d) 6 months

740. Under operators' licensing regulations, records of vehicle maintenance must be retained for at least 15 months at:

(a) the operator's home address
(b) the place where the vehicles are maintained
(c) the vehicle operating centre as specified on the 'O' licence
(d) the operator's registered business address

741. If an 'O' licence application is refused by a Licensing Authority the applicant has a right of appeal to:

(a) the High Court
(b) the Court of Appeal
(c) a magistrate's court
(d) the Transport Tribunal

742. An operator whose 'O' licence is revoked by an LA following convictions for heavy goods vehicle related offences has a right of appeal to:

(a) the Transport Tribunal
(b) the Court of Appeal
(c) a crown court
(d) the Goods Vehicle Centre, Swansea

743. When an 'O' licence has been suspended or curtailed the LA may direct that the vehicles in question are not to be used under any other 'O' licence for a period:

(a) not exceeding 3 months
(b) of a maximum of 6 months

(c) up to 9 months
(d) no longer than 12 months

744. If an 'O' licence holder is requested to produce his licence at a police station the maximum period which he may be given to do this is:

(a) 5 days
(b) 7 days
(c) 14 days
(d) 28 days

B15 Vehicle Costing

745. If a vehicle has fixed charges of £10,000 per year and covers 40,000 miles at a running cost of 25p per mile, what gross profit will be made if it is hired out at a rate of 60p per mile?

(a) 5 pence per mile
(b) 10 pence per mile
(c) 15 pence per mile
(d) 20 pence per mile

746. If a vehicle has 80 litres of fuel in its tank at the start of a journey and after covering 90 kilometres 50 litres are left, the average fuel consumption will be:

(a) 2.0km/litre
(b) 2.66km/litre
(c) 3.0km/litre
(d) 3.33km/litre

747. Which of the following is not usually a direct objective of vehicle costing activities?

(a) calculating drivers' wage rates
(b) calculating haulage rates
(c) planning efficient distribution operations
(d) planning capital investment programmes

748. Direct costs in haulage operations are defined as:

(a) the general administrative costs of a business

(b) the overhead costs of a haulage business
(c) costs that have been previously incorporated in the firm's budget
(d) costs which can be directly attributed to vehicle operations

749. Which of the following items would be considered a direct operating cost on a haulage business?

(a) advertising and publicity to attract new business
(b) the provision of directors' and management business cars
(c) local authority annual rates on haulage premises
(d) replacement tyres

750. When analysing goods vehicle costs, which of the following items would be identified as indirect costs?

(a) quarterly telephone accounts
(b) drivers' wages
(c) vehicle excise duty
(d) vehicle repairs and maintenance

751. An operator should be able to differentiate between the fixed and variable or running costs for vehicles. Which of the following is a fixed cost?

(a) unscheduled vehicle repairs
(b) regular inspection and servicing of vehicles
(c) local authority rates
(d) drivers' overnight accommodation on away journeys

752. A vehicle with total standing costs of £12,000 per year costs 20p per mile to run over 30,000 miles annually. To make 20 per cent gross profit the charge-out rate would have to be:

(a) 60p per mile
(b) 65p per mile
(c) 72p per mile
(d) 75p per mile

753. In a business, the direct costs are those which:

(a) are met directly from petty cash
(b) are paid immediately by cheque from the bank account
(c) relate directly to the administration of the business
(d) are directly attributable to a cost centre

754. A vehicle which is hired out at 60p per mile has fixed costs of £10,000 per year and costs 25p per mile over 40,000 miles annual running. What gross profit margin is made?

(a) 10 per cent
(b) 12 per cent
(c) 15 per cent
(d) 20 per cent

755. By increasing the miles run by a vehicle the total cost per mile will:

(a) reduce
(b) increase
(c) remain the same
(d) multiply by the daily distance covered

756. Weekly standing costs for a goods vehicle are £350 and the running cost is 35p per mile. If the vehicle covers 1,000 miles per week the operating cost per week is:

(a) £70
(b) £700
(c) £100
(d) £1,000

757. Costs which increase as the miles run by a vehicle increase are called:

(a) on-costs
(b) marginal costs
(c) variable costs
(d) establishment costs

758. An operator employs part-time drivers to operate an occasional service with a vehicle which would

otherwise be idle. The extra drivers' wages would be treated as:

(a) an indirect cost
(b) a marginal cost
(c) an on-cost
(d) a fixed cost

759. Vehicle running costs are usually determined on a basis of:

(a) cost per mile
(b) ton/miles
(c) fixed costs
(d) establishment costs

760. Which of the following items is identified as a running cost?

(a) training of staff
(b) advertising haulage services
(c) entertaining business customers
(d) vehicle fuel supplies

761. Which of the following would be classified as a variable cost?

(a) maintenance of depot premises
(b) maintenance of vehicles
(c) depreciation of vehicles
(d) insurance of vehicles

762. Which of the following costs is usually mileage based?

(a) staff and management salaries
(b) vehicle excise licences
(c) depreciation charges
(d) fuel and lubricating oil

763. What is the tyre cost per mile if a set of new tyres for a vehicle, excluding the spare, costs £1,500 and its anticipated life is 45,000 miles?

(a) 2.66p per mile
(b) 3.00p per mile

(c) 3.33p per mile
(d) 3.66p per mile

764. If a set of tyres for a vehicle costs £1,000 and has a life of 50,000 miles the cost per mile will be:

(a) 1p
(b) 2p
(c) 2.5p
(d) 3p

765. In quoting for a haulage contract which of the following items would be calculated as vehicle running costs?

(a) fuel only
(b) drivers' wages only
(c) both drivers' wages and holiday pay
(d) vehicle depreciation, tax and insurance

766. Which of the following items is a fixed vehicle cost?

(a) tyres
(b) vehicle insurance
(c) maintenance costs
(d) drivers' night-out expenses

767. Which of the following items would be classed among the standing costs of a haulage business?

(a) vehicle excise licences
(b) office staff salaries
(c) tyres
(d) bulk supplies of fuel and lubricants

768. In vehicle costing which of the following is usually classed as a standing cost?

(a) maintenance and repairs to vehicles
(b) life insurance on key employees
(c) vehicle depreciation
(d) fuel and oil supplies

769. It is important for hauliers to be able to distinguish between the fixed and variable costs in their operations. Which of the following items is a fixed cost?

(a) vehicle breakdown repairs
(b) premises insurance
(c) regular vehicle safety inspections
(d) drivers' night-out expenses

770. In vehicle costing calculations, which of the following items would be grouped towards the total standing costs for vehicles?

(a) depreciation, fuel and tyres
(b) vehicle servicing, lubricants, interest on capital
(c) vehicle insurance, drivers' bonus payments and fleet maintenance
(d) excise licences, vehicle insurance and drivers' basic wages

771. Which of the following would be regarded as a fixed expense in costing vehicle operations?

(a) fuel
(b) tyres
(c) servicing and repairs
(d) insurance premiums

772. Telephone charges incurred by a haulage company are classed as:

(a) running costs
(b) standing costs
(c) indirect costs
(d) direct costs

773. Which element of drivers' wages could be considered a fixed cost?

(a) basic wages
(b) overtime payments
(c) productivity bonuses
(d) meal and night-out expenses

774. When calculating haulage rates, which of the following would be classed as standing costs?

(a) vehicle insurance
(b) drivers' away-from-home expenses
(c) tyres
(d) diesel fuel

775. Although a goods vehicle may not be in use, it still incurs:

(a) running costs
(b) standing costs
(c) overhead costs
(d) marginal costs

776. A haulier looking to achieve 30 per cent gross profit on a vehicle for which the annual fixed costs are £9,000 and the running costs are 25p per mile for 45,000 miles per year would need to charge:

(a) 50p per mile
(b) 55p per mile
(c) 58.5p per mile
(d) 60p per mile

777. The term 'depreciation' used in vehicle costing is most simply defined as:

(a) the value of a vehicle at the end of its useful life
(b) the average value of a vehicle over its anticipated life
(c) the re-sale value of a vehicle at any point during its useful life
(d) a financial allowance to account for the deterioration of a vehicle throughout its life due mainly to wear and tear

778. The financial act of 'writing off' the value of an asset over its anticipated life is called:

(a) residual valuation
(b) depreciation
(c) revaluation
(d) appreciation

779. Inclusion of a provision for the depreciation of vehicles when compiling a haulage rate quotation would be under the heading of:

(a) standing costs
(b) variable costs
(c) overhead costs
(d) indirect costs

780. Some people prefer to calculate vehicle depreciation as a variable cost based on miles run but normally this is only justified:

(a) when a vehicle runs very high annual mileages
(b) when hire charges are calculated on a miles run basis
(c) when a vehicle is let out on contract hire
(d) when a vehicle only covers very low annual mileages

781. During a period of high inflation it would be more prudent for a haulier to calculate the depreciation of his vehicles on the basis of:

(a) current value
(b) original purchase price
(c) estimated new price
(d) replacement cost

782. An operator buys a lorry for £14,000 and estimates its resale value after 6 years to be £1,250; the original set of tyres cost £750. What amount must the operator set aside per annum by way of depreciation using the straight-line method?

(a) £1,500
(b) £2,000
(c) £2,200
(d) £2,500

783. An operator purchases a vehicle for £15,000 which he depreciates using the reducing balance method at a fixed 20 per cent per annum, setting him a resale value target at the end of two years of:

(a) £8,500
(b) £9,600
(c) £10,750

(d) £11,800

784. A vehicle costing £10,000 is estimated to have a useful life of 5 years and a residual value of £1,000. By the straight-line method the annual allowance for depreciation would be calculated as:

(a) £800
(b) £1,800
(c) £2,200
(d) £2,800

785. Using the straight-line method of calculation on a £16,000 vehicle with an anticipated life of 6 years and a residual value of £4,000, the annual depreciation charge would be:

(a) £1,500
(b) £2,000
(c) £2,500
(d) £3,000

786. Using the reducing balance method of calculation on a vehicle costing £15,000 with an anticipated life of 5 years and a 25 per cent write-down, the first year depreciation charge would be:

(a) £2,750
(b) £3,750
(c) £4,750
(d) £5,750

787. A new vehicle costing £69,500 with 6 wheels fitted with tyres worth £250 each is written down by the straight-line method to £12,000 over 7 years, resulting in an annual depreciation charge of:

(a) £6,800
(b) £7,800
(c) £8,000
(d) £9,800

788. If a vehicle purchased for £62,000 has a residual value of £6,000 after an estimated life of 7 years, by the

straight-line method of calculation the annual rate of depreciation would be:

(a) £6,200
(b) £7,500
(c) £8,000
(d) £8,500

789. A new vehicle costing £61,500 has 6 wheels with tyres worth £250 each. Calculating depreciation by the reducing balance method at 25 per cent per annum the value after two years would be:

(a) £33,750
(b) £23,750
(c) £19,750
(d) £36,750

790. By the reducing balance method of calculating depreciation for a vehicle costing £50,000 with an anticipated life of 5 years and a depreciation rate of 20 per cent per annum, the annual depreciation charge for the first year would be:

(a) £5,000
(b) £10,000
(c) £15,000
(d) £20,000

791. In a haulage operation which of the following items would be included under the heading of overhead costs of the business?

(a) the transport manager's salary
(b) vehicle excise licences
(c) drivers' basic wages
(b) lubricating oils

792. The general administrative costs of running a haulage business would be classed as:

(a) marginal costs
(b) variable costs
(c) overhead costs
(d) standing costs

793. The overhead costs of a road haulage business would include:

(a) vehicle insurance
(b) employer's share of pensions contributions
(c) interest on capital
(d) vehicle maintenance

794. In assessing the costs of running a haulage business, overheads are those which:

(a) are directly attributable to the vehicles
(b) cover the general administrative costs of the business
(c) arise directly from the ownership of the vehicles
(d) arise after vehicle fixed and variable costs have been recovered

795. Which of the following would be shown as an establishment charge in the costs of a haulage business?

(a) drivers' wages
(b) office stationery
(c) drivers' night-out expenses
(d) vehicle breakdown costs

796. If a haulage firm's costs are made up as follows what is the total of its overhead costs?

	£
general administrative costs	30,000
management salaries	50,000
vehicle maintenance, fuel and tyres	150,000
annual depreciation charges	70,000
driver's wages	90,000

(a) £50,000
(b) £80,000
(c) £150,000
(d) £310,000

797. A haulage fleet comprises 5 vehicles having the following carrying capacities: 2 vehicles of 5 tonnes each, 2 vehicles of 10 tonnes each and 1 vehicle of 20

tonnes. If the annual overhead costs, which amount to £15,000, are allocated to each of the vehicles on the basis of payload capacity, each of the 10 tonners would bear:

(a) £1,500
(b) £2,500
(c) £3,000
(d) £3,500

798. A 5-vehicle fleet covers the following average annual distance: 2 vehicles average 60,000 km each, 2 vehicles average 90,000 km each and 1 vehicle averages 150,000 km. If the firm's overhead costs, which total £13,500 annually, are allocated to the vehicles on a per kilometre basis, a vehicle averaging 50,000km per annum would carry an annual cost of:

(a) £500
(b) £1,000
(c) £1,500
(d) £2,500

B16 Methods of Payment

799. The term 'carriage forward' means that payment for the carriage of goods:

(a) has already been made by the consignor
(b) will be made by the consignee
(c) will be made later by the consignor
(d) will be made by the consignor's forwarding agent

800. One method by which a road haulage operator can encourage his customers to pay their accounts more promptly is to:

(a) offer them a trade discount
(b) offer them a cash discount
(c) permit them to pay by credit transfer
(d) permit them to pay in cash instead of by cheque

801. Which of the following constitutes a 'credit sale'?

(a) payment by cheque
(b) payment by Visa/Access card
(c) payment by giro cheque
(d) payment by postal order

802. Credit transfer is a method of payment for goods or services?

(a) by crossed cheque
(b) using a bank cheque card
(c) using Visa/Access or other credit card
(d) direct into the creditor's bank account

803. A haulier may demand payment in advance for the carriage of goods:

(a) only after goods have been delivered to the customer
(b) only within a limited period before he receives the goods
(c) only when the goods are received by him for delivery
(d) as soon as the contract is entered into

804. Which of the following defines a 'cash sale'?

(a) where immediate payment in full is made
(b) where payment is made in cash
(c) where payment is by either cheque or cash
(d) payment where a receipt rather than an invoice is required

805. When a budget account credit arrangement is agreed whereby goods may be purchased up to so many times a regular monthly repayment, who actually makes the loan?

(a) a finance company
(b) a bank
(c) the retailer
(d) a credit card organisation

806. If a purchaser fails to pay for goods or services within a stipulated period, the vendor may charge interest on the money owed:

(a) under no circumstances whatever
(b) under any circumstances if he believes the purchaser will pay
(c) providing the purchaser is notified in writing that interest will be charged within 30 days of the account becoming due for payment
(d) providing the purchaser was notified of the fact in writing at the time the purchase was made

807. A footnote on an invoice that payment terms are '2.5 per cent one month' means that the recipient:

(a) will have to pay 2.5 per cent interest per month for each month the account remains unpaid
(b) may deduct 2.5 per cent from the total amount owing if payment is made within one month
(c) must pay at least 2.5 per cent of the total amount due within one month
(d) must pay the total amount of the account less 2.5 per cent within one month

B17 Methods of Operating

808. Which of the following organisations provides a 'groupage' service?

(a) the Road Haulage Association
(b) the British Institute of Freight Forwarders
(c) the National Association of Warehouse Keepers
(d) a freight forwarder

809. A principal haulier can pass liability claims for lost or damaged loads to the sub-contractors who transported them.

(a) True
(b) False

810. In haulage industry terms a 'sub-contractor' is defined as:

(a) an agent who undertakes sub-contracted commissions for a principal
(b) a haulage contractor who sub-contracts work to other hauliers

(c) a haulier who undertakes work on behalf of the original contractor
(d) a forwarding agent who arranges transport and prepares the necessary documentation and insurance

811. In connection with the normal business carried out by firms operating as freight forwarders, which of the following statements is correct?

(a) export documentation can only be lodged with HM Customs and Excise by an approved freight forwarder
(b) use of a freight forwarder for customs clearance is not compulsory in the UK
(c) freight forwarders must hold a certificate of competence before they can offer their services
(d) freight forwarders should only be used when consigning exports beyond the EC

812. Groupage is a term used to describe the activity:

(a) where individual consignments are consolidated into a larger single consignment for a trunk haul often by trailer or container
(b) where transport operators combine to share common premises
(c) where a freight forwarder integrates deliveries for a group of companies
(d) where a haulier specialises in combined deliveries to a particular group of countries

813. The function of a transport clearing house is:

(a) to arrange Customs clearance for vehicles arriving at a port with import or export consignments
(b) to arrange clearance sales of bankruptcy stocks
(c) to arrange clearance of vehicles prohibited by DTp examiners
(d) to arrange for goods to be transported by sub-contracted hauliers

814. A haulier offering a regular trailer service for the transport of small consignments to specified

destinations where the loads are broken-down for local distribution:

(a) provides a factoring service
(b) is a haulage clearing house
(c) operates a warehousing and distribution service
(d) provides a groupage service

815. The transportation system whereby a number of small consignments are consolidated into a unit load is called:

(a) containerisation
(b) groupage
(c) cabotage
(d) trunking

816. In haulage terms, if haulier A contracts to carry goods for B and he in turn sub-contracts the work to C and the goods are damaged in transit:

(a) B should sue A who was the original contractor
(b) B should sue C who was the sub-contractor who carried the goods
(c) B can sue both A and C since both were party to the movement
(d) B will rely on A to sue C to recover damages

817. If after a haulier has sub-contracted work to another operator the goods are lost in transit the original haulier is:

(a) fully liable to the customer for the full value of the loss
(b) not liable to the customer for losses brought about by the action of the sub-contractor
(c) only liable for the loss if the sub-contractor fails to compensate the customer
(d) not liable if he advised the customer that he was sub-contracting the work to another haulier

818. In road haulage operations a clearing house is:

(a) an organisation which arranges clearance of goods through Customs

(b) an agency from which hauliers can hire extra drivers and other staff
(c) a firm which organises sub-contract hauliers to move customer's goods
(d) the system whereby banks clear each other's cheques

819. A haulier providing a regular service of collecting small consignments, and combining them into bulk loads for transport to specified destinations where the bulk loads are broken down for local distribution of the individual consignments, undertakes the activities of:

(a) consolidation and break-bulk
(b) warehousing and distribution
(c) logistics
(d) load scheduling

820. An organisation set up specifically to organise the movement of loads by the use of sub-contracted hauliers is known as:

(a) a third-part operator
(b) a contract haulier
(c) a transport clearing house
(d) a distribution contractor

821. The consolidation of individual consignments into bulk unit loads to be trunked to a common destination is known as:

(a) logistics management
(b) load scheduling
(c) groupage
(d) contract distribution

822. In road transport, firms operating as clearing houses provide a service:

(a) arranging to clear vehicle prohibition notices
(b) clearing surplus and bankruptcy stocks by organising bargain sales
(c) arranging to move loads by sub-contracting to small hauliers

(d) arranging insurance, documentation and Customs clearance of transport documents

823. In road haulage operations, a firm which arranges with consignors to have their loads transported by sub-contract hauliers is called:

(a) a public carrier
(b) a national carrier
(c) a ccntract haulier
(d) a clearing house

B18 Vehicle Excise Duty and Trade Plates

824. The minimum period for which a vehicle excise licence may be obtained is:

(a) 3 months
(b) 6 months
(c) 9 months
(d) 12 months

825. As a general rule vehicle excise duty for heavy goods vehicles is payable according to:

(a) their unladen weight
(b) whether they are rigid or articulated
(c) their gross weight and number of axles
(d) the number of axles

826. Where vehicle excise duty is originally paid for 12 months but is no longer required after 9 months, application for a refund of duty for each complete month remaining on the licence may be made.

(a) True
(b) False

827. Which of the following classes of vehicle is not exempt from excise duty?

(a) electrically-propelled vehicles
(b) farmers' goods vehicles
(c) fire service vehicles

(d) vehicles en route to a place by prior appointment for annual test

828. If a vehicle owner is convicted of keeping a vehicle on the road without a current excise licence in force he may be fined and ordered to pay back duty for a period during which the vehicle was unlicensed.

(a) True
(b) False

829. A goods vehicle with an unladen weight of 1,550kg is liable for excise duty based on:

(a) its gross plated weight
(b) its unladen weight
(c) the private/light goods (PLG) duty rate
(d) the number of axles

830. Vehicle excise duty payable for an articulated goods vehicle combination with a gross train weight of 12,000kg is based on:

(a) the unladen weight and the number of axles
(b) its gross train weight only
(c) its gross train weight and the number of axles on the tractive unit
(d) its gross train weight and the total number of axles

831. Excise duty is chargeable in respect of goods-carrying trailers in which of the following circumstances?

(a) where the trailer exceeds 4 tonnes gross weight and is towed by a vehicle exceeding 12 tonnes gross weight
(b) where the trailer exceeds 12 tonnes gross weight and is towed by a vehicle exceeding 12 tonnes gross weight
(c) where the trailer exceeds 2 tonnes gross weight and is towed by a vehicle not exceeding 12 tonnes gross weight
(d) where the trailer exceeds 1 tonne gross weight and is towed by a vehicle exceeding 4 tonnes gross weight

832. A goods vehicle with an unladen weight of 1,625kg will be subject to excise duty on the basis of:

(a) its gross plated weight
(b) the PLG rate
(c) its unladen weight
(d) the rigid goods vehicle rate

833. Additional excise duty payable when a rigid goods vehicle draws a trailer exceeding 4,000kg gross weight applies when the gross weight of the towing vehicle exceeds:

(a) 1,525kg
(b) 7,500kg
(c) 12,000kg
(d) 16,260kg

834. For which of the following vehicle combinations may excise duty be paid for operation at a gross train weight of 38 tonnes?

(a) a tractive unit with 3 axles and a semi-trailer with 1 axle
(b) a tractive unit with 3 axles and a semi-trailer with 2 axles
(c) a tractive unit with 2 axles and a semi-trailer with 1 axle
(d) a tractive unit with 2 axles and a semi-trailer with 2 axles

835. If an operator leaves a broken-down vehicle with an expired excise licence parked on the road he is:

(a) not liable to be prosecuted because no offence was committed
(b) liable to prosecution because he committed the offence of being the keeper of an unlicensed vehicle on the road
(c) not liable to prosecution because the vehicle was there only temporarily due to the break-down
(d) not liable to prosecution if he can prove it was genuinely broken- down

836. The law requires the display of a vehicle excise licence disc:

(a) in the windscreen where it can easily be seen
(b) in the windscreen on the nearside
(c) in the windscreen or a nearside window
(d) in a window to the front of the driver's seat

837. If Customs and Excise officers wish to examine a goods vehicle their principal concern will be to ensure that:

(a) the correct amount of vehicle excise duty has been paid
(b) the operator is registered for VAT and makes proper returns
(c) the fuel in the tank is duty-paid diesel not gas oil
(d) the driver is carrying a proper record of the weight of his load

838. The maximum period for which a trade licence may be taken out is:

(a) 6 months
(b) 12 months
(c) 2 years
(d) 4 years

839. Application for a trade licence has to be made to:

(a) the Department of Trade and Industry
(b) the Driver and Vehicle Licensing Centre, Swansea
(c) a local Vehicle Registration Office
(d) a local office of HM Customs and Excise

840. The maximum number of trade licences permitted for a transport operator carrying out its own vehicle servicing and maintenance is:

(a) 1
(b) 2
(c) 4
(d) not restricted

841. On the grant of a trade licence a pair of trade plates is issued for attachment to vehicles used under the licence. The plate containing the triangular licence must be:

(a) displayed on the front of the vehicle
(b) displayed at the rear of the vehicle
(c) displayed in the windscreen
(d) attached so as to cover the existing registration plate

842. Trade plates issued under a trade licence are made up with:

(a) black letters and numbers on a red background
(b) black letters and numbers on a white background
(c) red letters and numbers on a black background
(d) red letters and numbers on a white background

843. A trade licence issued for use on vehicles:

(a) must be attached to the trade plate carried at the rear of the vehicle
(b) must be attached to the trade plate carried at the front of the vehicle
(c) must be displayed in the windscreen of the vehicle in use
(d) need not be displayed provided the plates are attached to the vehicle

844. If the grant of a trade licence is refused an appeal can be made in writing within 28 days to:

(a) the local Vehicle Registration Office
(b) a magistrate's court
(c) the Secretary of State for Transport
(d) the head of the Driver and Vehicle Licensing Centre, Swansea

845. Which of the following activities would be constitute legal use of a trade licence?

(a) to permit temporary use of a vehicle with an expired excise licence
(b) to road test an unlicensed vehicle after repair
(c) to enable a perishable load to be transferred to an unlicensed vehicle following a breakdown
(d) to enable a person interested in promoting publicity for a new vehicle to drive it before it is licensed

846. A vehicle being operated under a trade licence:

(a) must not be used for the carriage of goods
(b) may carry a load when this is necessary to demonstrate the capabilities of the vehicle
(c) may carry a load provided it belongs to the trade licence holder
(d) may carry a load but only between points specified in the licence

847. A service vehicle used by a haulier for towing broken-down vehicles and collecting vehicle components may be used under a trade licence.

(a) True
(b) False

848. Which of the following categories of passenger may be legally carried on a vehicle operated under a trade licence?

(a) a person in a broken-down vehicle being towed
(b) a prospective customer assessing the capabilities of the vehicle
(c) a friend of the licence holder being given a lift home
(d) an employee of the licence holder being given a lift home

849. Under which of the following circumstances would the holder of a trade licence be acting unlawfully?

(a) by using it on a recovery vehicle
(b) by failing to display a current 'O' licence disc on a goods vehicle in addition to the trade plates on the vehicle
(c) by allowing a vehicle used under the licence to carry goods for demonstration purposes
(d) by allowing the vehicle to remain parked on a public road when not in use

850. Which of the following uses is not permitted under the terms of a trade licence?

(a) delivering a load while road-testing a vehicle following annual test preparation

(b) collecting a new vehicle from the bodybuilder
(c) demonstrating a vehicle to a prospective purchaser
(d) collecting components for the vehicle from the supplier

6: Typical Questions - Goods International Examination

851. Which of the following countries is a signatory to the AETR agreement?

(a) East Germany
(b) Poland
(c) Hungary
(d) Bulgaria

852. How many hours can be driven in the current week by a driver operating under the EC drivers' hours rules (ie EC 3820/85) who drove for 56 hours during the previous week?

(a) 48 hours
(b) 56 hours
(c) 34 hours
(d) 45 hours

853. Under the AETR drivers' hours rules the daily driving limit of 450km applicable to vehicle combinations exceeding 20 tonnes permissible maximum weight:

(a) must not be exceeded in any circumstances
(b) may be exceeded providing daily driving does not exceed 8 hours
(c) may be exceeded providing the vehicle has a calibrated tachograph which is used by the driver for record keeping purposes
(d) may be exceeded providing daily driving does not exceed 9 hours

854. The daily limit on driving time for a driver of a 38-tonne vehicle on an international journey operating under AETR rules is:

(a) 8 hours
(b) 9 hours
(c) 10 hours
(d) 11 hours

855. The driver of a goods vehicle on an international road haulage journey from the UK to Yugoslavia is restricted by the AETR agreement to a maximum weekly driving limit of:

(a) 46 hours
(b) 48 hours
(c) 54 hours
(d) 57 hours

856. On an international journey, to which of the following countries would a UK driver of an over-3.5 tonne vehicle be subject to the AETR drivers' hours rules?

(a) Hungary
(b) Poland
(c) Switzerland
(d) Sweden

857. Drivers operating under the AETR agreement must take a minimum weekly rest period of:

(a) 24 hours
(b) 24 hours immediately preceded or followed by a daily rest period
(c) 29 hours
(d) 29 hours immediately preceded or followed by a daily rest period

858. When travelling on international journeys a British driver must ensure his tachograph always shows the official time in the UK.

(a) True
(b) False

859. An EC approved tachograph used in a goods vehicle on an international journey from Croydon to Milan must:

(a) be switched off when the driver is taking a statutory break

(b) be kept operating only while the vehicle is travelling on the road but not during the cross-channel ferry crossing
(c) be kept operating continuously from the time the driver takes over the vehicle until he returns to base
(d) be operated only while the driver is at the wheel of the vehicle

860. If a tachograph breaks down on an international journey it must be repaired en route if, counting from the day of the breakdown, the vehicle is unable to return to base within:

(a) 2 days
(b) 3 days
(c) 5 days
(d) 7 days

861. When driving under EC drivers' hours rules on an international journey the driver must have with him and be able to produce his tachograph charts for:

(a) the previous 2 weeks
(b) the previous 7 days
(c) the current week and his last driving day in the previous week
(d) all driving since his last international journey

862. A period permit issued under the French bilateral agreement permits:

(a) 1 return journey only to or through France
(b) 1 return journey to France within a specified period
(c) a fixed number of journeys to France within a specified period
(d) an unlimited number of journeys during the period of its validity

863. Two types of permit are available under bilateral agreements:

(a) journey and period permits

(b) bilateral and multilateral permits
(c) EEC and ECMT permits
(d) piggy-back and road/rail certificates

864. A UK haulage vehicle carrying an international load for delivery in Lisbon and travelling via the Dover-Calais cross-channel ferry would require road haulage permits for:

(a) France and Spain
(b) France, Spain and Portugal
(c) Portugal only
(d) France, Andorra and Spain

865. A haulier requested by a customer to deliver goods to West Germany would need to make application for a journey permit to:

(a) the West Germany Embassy in London
(b) the Department of Transport in London
(c) the Road Haulage Association
(d) the International Road Freight Office

866. A loaded goods vehicle with a permissible laden weight not exceeding 6 tonnes travelling via France on an international journey to Luxembourg would need:

(a) a French bilateral journey permit
(b) a Luxembourg bilateral journey permit
(c) no permit as the operation is exempt
(d) an ECMT road haulage permit

867. A driver travels from Dover to Ostend on a cross-channel ferry with a delivery to be made 32 km from the port. For this journey he would require:

(a) a road/rail certificate
(b) an ECMT road haulage permit
(c) a Belgian bilateral journey permit
(d) no permit as the operation is exempt

868. The Goods Vehicles (International Road Haulage Permits) Regulations 1975 make it illegal to undertake a road haulage journey from the UK without a permit to or through:

(a) the Netherlands and Luxembourg
(b) Belgium and the Netherlands
(c) France and West Germany
(d) Switzerland and East Germany

869. The purpose of bilateral permits issued in the UK is to enable goods vehicles to make international journeys:

(a) to and from another contracting state starting from the UK
(b) on return only from another contracting state
(c) between 2 contracting states excluding the UK
(d) between 3 or more contracting states

870. A UK own-account operator who delivers a load of his own goods to a destination in France under an own-account document (in lieu of a road haulage permit) is offered a return load from France. What is the legal position?

(a) he may carry the load if the goods are for use by his own company in the UK only
(b) he may carry the load so long as it does not involve delivery in France
(c) he may accept the load so long as arrangements were made before he left the UK
(d) he may not accept the return load under any circumstances

871. What type of permit would a UK operator need to undertake haulage operations through France, Spain and Portugal?

(a) a bilateral road haulage permit
(b) an EC journey permit
(c) a co-operation quota permit
(d) an EC or ECMT multilateral permit

872. The system of EC permits allows a UK haulier to undertake international haulage journeys:

(a) between the UK and only one other contracting state
(b) between any number of EC member states

(c) within the boundaries of any EC member state
(d) across the whole of the European mainland

873. ECMT road haulage permits are issued to cover road haulage operations between:

(a) the UK and other EC member states
(b) the 19 contracting states to the Euro Conference of Transport Ministers
(c) the UK and non-EC member states
(d) the UK and non-EC state members of the ECMT

874. Use of the road/rail services operated by French and West Germany railways:

(a) allows hauliers to transit these states without road haulage permits
(b) saves Customs clearance formalities at international borders
(c) exempts the journey from the use of Community Transit documentation
(d) avoids the need for CMR Insurance cover

875. Road/rail certificates for permit-free transit on West German railways will not be issued by the International Road Freight Office until:

(a) vehicle/trailer measurements have been notified to the IRFO
(b) the transit booking has been confirmed to the IRFO
(c) weight tickets are provided for vehicle/trailer combinations
(d) cheque payments have been cleared through the applicant's bank

876. In road haulage terms, cabotage is:

(a) an illegal act not permitted in any European state
(b) permitted where valid EC multilateral permits have been issued
(c) illegal only in France, West Germany and Italy
(d) permitted provided a valid ECMT multilateral permit is held

877. Which of the following haulage operations carried out with a UK registered road haulage vehicle would be defined as cabotage?

(a) Collect from Shannon and deliver to Lyon
(b) Collect from Dusseldorf and deliver to Bordeaux
(c) Collect from Rheims and deliver to Montpellier
(d) Collect from Croydon and deliver to Cherbourg

878. If a UK haulier collects and delivers a load between the following European cities, which of the journeys would be classed as cabotage?

(a) Rheims and Rotterdam
(b) Bremerhaven and London
(c) Brussels and Liege
(d) Larne and Cork

879. Initial application to the International Road Freight Office for a road haulage permit must be accompanied by which of the following documents?

(a) a copy of a current CMR insurance certificate
(b) a copy of the TIR approval certificate for the vehicle/trailer
(c) the applicant's international 'O' licence
(d) the applicant's international professional competence qualification

880. Unless otherwise exempt, the Goods Vehicles (International Road Haulage Permits) Regulations 1975 make it an offence to use a UK vehicle without a valid haulage permit on journeys to or through which of the following countries?

(a) the Netherlands
(b) Italy
(c) Turkey
(d) Yugoslavia

881. Allocation of bilateral road haulage permits is made:

(a) 3-monthly
(b) 6-monthly
(c) 12-monthly

(d) 24-monthly

882. A road haulage permit issued by the International Road Freight Office must be returned by the operator:

(a) within 7 days after use or, if unused, the expiry date
(b) within 15 days after use or, if unused, the expiry date
(c) within 30 days after use or, if unused, the expiry date
(d) in any case no later than the date of expiry

883. Among other matters, provisions of European Community Directive 2005/62:

(a) exempt certain road haulage traffic from quotas and permits
(b) introduce the Community quota system for the allocation of permits
(c) apply a system of rate tariffs throughout the Community
(d) authorise the use of certain rail systems for road vehicle transit

884. UK hauliers require EC multilateral road haulage permits:

(a) to undertake international journeys from the UK to an EC state
(b) to undertake tramping operations between member states of the EC
(c) to transit EC countries to pick up loads from outside the EC
(d) to authorise unaccompanied trailer operations to the EC

885. The issue of an EC multilateral permit provides authority to:

(a) undertake both haulage and own-account operations to the EC
(b) send unaccompanied trailer traffic to the EC
(c) undertake international journeys outside the EC

(d) undertake tramping haulage between EC member states

886. Multilateral road haulage permits issued under the auspices of the ECMT are valid for journeys between EC member states and to:

(a) Bulgaria
(b) Czechoslovakia
(c) Hungary
(d) Yugoslavia

887. An ECMT removals permit permits the holder to:

(a) undertake tramping haulage between ECMT contracting states
(b) operate removals with specialised staff/ equipment between ECMT states
(c) undertake cabotage operations within ECMT contracting states
(d) carry return loads of furniture from Europe

888. ECMT road haulage permits are valid for haulage operations in:

(a) EC member states only
(b) member states of the European Conference of Ministers of Transport
(c) both EC and Comecon member states
(d) both EC and EFTA member states

889. EC multilateral permits covering haulage operations only are valid for a maximum of one year and cover:

(a) only one vehicle at a time
(b) any number of vehicles operated on international journeys
(c) only vehicles specified by registration number on the permit
(d) all of the holder's fleet specified on his international 'O' licence

890. An EC multilateral journey permit can be used by a road haulage operator for:

(a) a maximum of 1 return journey in a month
(b) a maximum of 50 return journeys within 1 year
(c) no more than 2 vehicle journeys at any one time
(d) an unlimited number of journeys within 1 calendar year

891. When travelling on an international journey the original of the vehicle registration document must be carried on the vehicle.

(a) True
(b) False

892. UK vehicles travelling abroad are required to display a national identification plate:

(a) in all circumstances
(b) only within the European Community
(c) only if their gross weight exceeds 3.5 tonnes
(d) when operating for hire and reward only

893. A person can obtain an international driving permit from the RAC or AA provided he/she has a current valid driving licence and:

(a) lives in the UK and is at least 18 years of age
(b) lives in the UK and is at least 21 years of age
(c) can show that there have been no driving convictions in the past year
(d) is a paid-up member of the AA/RAC/RSAC

894. For undertaking a journey to which of the following countries would it be necessary for a UK driver to have a visa in addition to a passport?

(a) Portugal
(b) Bulgaria
(c) Yugoslavia
(d) Hungary

895. To enter which of the following countries would an international haulage driver need to obtain a visa?

(a) Greece
(b) Turkey

(c) Romania
(d) Finland

896. Which of the following countries will accept a British driving licence provided that a translation of the licence is also carried?

(a) Italy
(b) Spain
(c) Portugal
(d) Turkey

897. Yugoslavia imposes a road tax on vehicles in transit through its territory based on:

(a) gross weight and the distance travelled in the country
(b) payload tonnage and the length of stay in the country
(c) kilometres travelled within the country
(d) a tonnage rate for the amount of payload

898. At the frontier of which of the following countries is a kilometre tax payable on diesel-powered vehicles based on their configuration and gross weight?

(a) Greece
(b) Turkey
(c) Portugal
(d) Sweden

899. Which of the following countries imposes a road transport tax for loaded vehicles with a maximum payload capacity over 5 tonnes travelling to or through its territory?

(a) Denmark
(b) Austria
(c) East Germany
(d) Eire

900. France sets a limit on the amount of fuel that can be imported in the fuel tanks of a goods vehicle when entering its territory before excise duty is payable.

(a) True
(b) False

901. The maximum amount of road fuel that can be imported duty free in a vehicle entering the Federal Republic of Germany is:

(a) 50 litres
(b) 100 litres
(c) 200 litres
(d) unspecified

902. Before additional duties become payable, the amount of road fuel that can be imported in vehicle running tanks according to an EC Directive is:

(a) 50 litres
(b) 100 litres
(c) 200 litres
(d) 250 litres

903. The Customs and Excise system whereby official control is exercised and records kept of goods to be exported abroad is known as:

(a) prior export clearance
(b) a simplified trade procedure
(c) pre-entry
(d) export trade recording

904. Which of the following organisations would issue a 'house' bill for an international consolidated load despatched from the UK?

(a) the cross-channel ferry operator
(b) the customer's appointed freight agent
(c) HM Customs and Excise at the port of exit
(d) the International Road Freight Office

905. Which of the following categories of goods need not be pre-entered with HM Customs and Excise prior to export abroad?

(a) goods covered by the common agriculture policy (CAP)

(b) goods exported from a Customs and Excise bonded warehouse
(c) goods shipped under the simplified clearance procedure (SCP)
(d) goods for which an export licence is required

906. Which of the following categories of goods must be pre-entered with HM Customs and Excise?

(a) exports from a Customs and Excise bonded warehouse
(b) export loads comprising hazardous substances
(c) consolidated loads consigned for export
(d) goods shipped under the simplified clearance procedure (SCP)

907. The copy of the Single Administrative Document (SAD) used for the declaration of imported goods is:

(a) copy 2
(b) copy 4
(c) copy 6
(d) copy 7

908. The pre-entry system under the SCP allows an exporter with a CRN to present the SAD document within a time limit of:

(a) 5 days
(b) 7 days
(c) 10 days
(d) 14 days

909. The Customs and Excise procedure for exporters who have a Customs-registered number to provide statistical information is called:

(a) the simplified clearance procedure (SCP)
(b) the Community Transit (CT) procedure
(c) pre-entry
(d) CRN entry

910. The introduction of the single administrative document (SAD) in Customs procedures means that:

(a) a single document can be used for worldwide export and import purposes
(b) a single document can be used as an export/import declaration for trade with non-EC countries
(c) a common single document is used for export and import declarations throughout all EC member states
(d) the Community Transit (CT) system no longer applies to export consignments within the EC

911. Under the SCP pre-shipment advice requirement for export consignments HM Customs accept a CMR note, an FTA own-account document, or:

(a) a Customs form C273
(b) a Community Transit form T1
(c) a carnet de passage en douane
(d) Copy 2 of the SAD

912. The main reason for HM Customs requiring pre-entry of exports is to:

(a) provide information for statistical purposes and to control the movement of prohibited goods
(b) ensure that the haulier has the correct documentation for an international movement of an export consignment
(c) ensure that the exporter has established a proper outlet for his goods abroad
(d) ensure that correct levels of export duties are charged

913. Exporters who have registered and been allocated a Customs-registered number (CRN) may use the:

(a) simplified clearance procedure (SCP)
(b) TIR carnet procedure
(c) Community Transit (CT) procedure
(d) Customs commercial documentation procedure

914. A UK haulier on a journey to Greece via West Germany, Austria and Yugoslavia would need to use which of the following Customs systems?

(a) the Greek national transit system
(b) Transports Internationale Routier (TIR)
(c) Community Transit
(d) ATA temporary importation

915. For which of the following countries would the driver on an international journey be expected to have a form EUR 1 in respect of the goods carried?

(a) Hungary
(b) Norway
(c) Italy
(d) Romania

916. The acceptance of transit guarantee vouchers when using the full Community Transit system is subject to the approval of the guarantor by the:

(a) Department of Trade and Industry
(b) Department of Transport
(c) International Road Transport Union (IRU)
(d) HM Customs and Excise

917. Firms moving goods between the UK and other EC member states can avoid having to lodge individual deposits to cover possible Customs claims if they use:

(a) authenticated certificates of origin
(b) Community Transit guarantee vouchers
(c) CMR consignment notes
(d) EUR 1 movement certificates

918. If a hazardous load is to be shipped on a cross-channel ferry which of the following documents must be presented to the ferry operator?

(a) the CMR consignment note
(b) the bilateral road haulage permit covering the journey
(c) a SITPRO dangerous goods shipping note
(d) an ADR vehicle approval certificate

919. Single Administrative Documents used as transit documents in conjunction with the Community Transit system must be lodged at:

(a) the local Customs and Excise office
(b) the office of departure
(c) the office of destination
(d) the International Road Freight Office

920. A vehicle moving goods from the UK via Italy and overland to Greece must use which of the following Customs systems?

(a) the Greek national transit system
(b) Community Transit from the UK through to Greece
(c) Community Transit to Italy and TIR from Italy to Greece
(d) TIR for the whole journey

921. Community Transit may be used for international journeys from the EC to which of the following non-Community countries?

(a) Austria
(b) Sweden
(c) Norway
(d) East Germany

922. A Community Transit T2 declaration indicates that the goods in question are:

(a) in free circulation within EC member states
(b) imported from countries outside the EC
(c) not in free circulation within EC member states
(d) in free circulation in Spain and Portugal

923. Community transit guarantee vouchers are only valid if provided by:

(a) the AA or RAC
(b) a Customs approved guarantor
(c) the Export Credits Guarantee Department (ECGD)
(d) the exporter's bankers

924. Community transit guarantee vouchers are valid in which of the following non-EC countries?

(a) East Germany

(b) Sweden
(c) Czechoslovakia
(d) Switzerland

925. HM Customs will accept guarantees given under Community Transit if they are provided by:

(a) the Department of Trade and Industry
(b) the International Road Transport Union (IRU)
(c) the Road Haulage Association
(d) the Export Credits Guarantee Department (ECGD)

926. A Community Transit guarantee voucher:

(a) exempts the exporter from Customs duty
(b) saves exporters making individual deposits to cover Customs duty claims
(c) guarantees transit of goods across frontiers without Customs inspection
(d) guarantees payment for export goods by the customer

927. Exporters consigning goods from the UK to the EC can avoid the need to lodge customs deposits by using the system of:

(a) Community Transit T2 declarations
(b) TIR instead of Community Transit
(c) Community Transit Article 41 procedure
(d) Community Transit guarantee vouchers

928. The Community Transit procedure which facilitates movement of goods within the EC also covers two non-Community member states:

(a) Austria and Switzerland
(b) Albania and Yugoslavia
(c) East Germany and Czechoslovakia
(d) Norway and Sweden

929. Under the Community Transit guarantee system, flat rate guarantee vouchers can be obtained from the guarantor each providing cover up to:

(a) 2,500 units of account

(b) 3,000 units of account
(c) 5,000 units of account
(d) 6,000 units of account

930. To be sure he gets paid, if a foreign customer defaults, an exporter will obtain:

(a) an ECGD certificate
(b) an ECMT permit
(c) a carnet de passage en douane
(d) CMR insurance cover

931. Certain operations under the full CT procedure do not need to be covered by guarantee. These include:

(a) where the consignment is shipped by both road and sea
(b) where the load is carried by a single vehicle for the whole journey
(c) when a CMR consignment note is in force
(d) transit between a UK office of departure and the first office of transit

932. An EC member state wishing to verify that goods being consigned for export are in free circulation within the Community would accept as proof:

(a) an official certificate of origin
(b) copy 4 of the SAD showing T2 status
(c) the haulier's CMR note
(d) copy 4 of the SAD showing T1 status

933. Which of the following would be used to establish the origin of goods made and exported from the UK to the EC but which is not accepted as a transit document?

(a) Form T5 control copy
(b) T2L procedure
(c) T1 declaration on the SAD
(d) T2 declaration on the SAD

934. An international road haulier should take out insurance cover against:

(a) consequential loss of goods en route

(b) CMR liabilities
(c) goods in transit risks
(d) Customs claims for unpaid duty

935. A UK haulier transporting a hire or reward load from Leeds to Bordeaux via the cross-channel ferries would be subject to CMR Convention conditions:

(a) only if he voluntarily agrees to accept the conditions
(b) only for that part of the journey on mainland Europe
(c) for the whole of the journey
(d) only if he has taken out CMR liability insurance cover

936. When transporting goods by road for hire or reward on an international journey, goods in transit insurance should be obtained:

(a) to cover maximum liabilities of £800 per tonne
(b) to cover maximum liabilities of £1,200 per tonne
(c) to cover the current level of CMR liability
(d) to cover liabilities in the currency of the country of destination

937. Customs status T1 would apply to goods exported from the UK to other EC states which are:

(a) not in free circulation within the Community
(b) in free circulation within the Community
(c) subject to special rates of import duty
(d) allowed entry free of duty in any country

938. A loaded semi-trailer despatched unaccompanied to France for delivery would have to carry which of the following documents?

(a) a copy of Community Transit form T2
(b) an ATA carnet
(c) a carnet de passage en douane
(d) a TIR carnet

939. A full 8-part SAD set would be used for which of the following purposes?

(a) for export, Community Transit and import purposes
(b) for export declaration purposes only
(c) for import declaration purposes only
(d) for Community Transit purposes only

940. An exporter who does not wish to become directly involved with export procedures for his goods can put the whole operation into the hands of:

(a) the Freight Transport Association
(b) the Road Haulage Association
(c) the Chartered Institute of Transport
(d) a firm of freight forwarders

941. The RHA and FTA act as guarantors for liability for Customs duty on goods transported outside the EC by issuing:

(a) TIR carnets
(b) ATA carnets
(c) carnets de passage en douane
(d) ATP carnets

942. The SAD form in use throughout the Community comprises an 8-part set, certain copies of which remain in the country of dispatch while other copies travel forward with the goods. How many copies travel forward?

(a) copies 1 to 3
(b) copies 3 to 6
(c) copies 2 to 6
(d) copies 4 to 8

943. The document used to permit goods vehicles to pass through international frontiers, other than EC member states, without Customs examination is called:

(a) a Community Transit consignment note
(b) a TIR carnet
(c) a CMR consignment note
(d) a SAD form

944. **For non-Community road haulage movements the Community Transit system is replaced by:**

(a) the AETR agreement
(b) the TIR convention
(c) the CMR convention
(d) the ATP convention

945. **TIR in the context of road transport is an international agreement:**

(a) to allow vehicles to cross national frontiers without Customs examination
(b) to control the movement of hazardous substances by road
(c) to control the movement of perishable goods by road
(d) to require international hauliers to be correctly covered by insurance

946. **The TIR certificate of approval issued in respect of vehicles must be renewed:**

(a) annually
(b) bi-annually
(c) every 4 years
(d) every 6 years

947. **Vehicles operating internationally under the TIR convention must carry:**

(a) a valid TIR carnet only
(b) a valid TIR carnet and a certificate of approval for the vehicle
(c) a valid TIR carnet, a certificate of approval for the vehicle and TIR plates front and rear
(d) a valid TIR carnet and TIR plates front and rear

948. **A TIR carnet is a document accepted as:**

(a) a bond against any Customs duties payable at frontier crossings
(b) evidence that a bilateral road haulage permit exists for the journey
(c) evidence of insurance cover for international road haulage journeys

(d) evidence that the vehicle meets TIR approval standards

949. Unless an emergency situation arises, a driver should not break the TIR seals on his vehicle during the journey.

(a) True
(b) False

950. A TIR carnet contains a number of pages (volets) depending on the number of borders to be crossed on an international journey, but each full carnet covers:

(a) a single outward load only
(b) a single outward and return load
(c) any number of outward journeys within the period of validity
(d) any number of outward and return journeys within its validity

951. The main purpose of a TIR carnet is to ensure that the vehicle and load:

(a) can be readily examined by Customs officials en-route
(b) can be Customs sealed during transit to prevent removals from or additions to the load
(c) are correctly documented for export/import duty purposes
(d) are correctly valued for international transport insurance purposes

952. To which of the following bodies is application made for inspection of vehicles for TIR approval purposes?

(a) the International Road Freight Office
(b) the Department of Transport, Goods Vehicle Centre, Swansea
(c) the clerk to the Licensing Authority for the Traffic Area in which the vehicle is available for inspection
(d) the manager of the nearest DTp Goods Vehicle Test Station

953. Once a vehicle has received a TIR Certificate of Approval:

(a) re-certification is necessary if it is transferred to a new owner
(b) the Certificate can be transferred to a new owner without the vehicle having to be examined again for TIR approval purposes
(c) the vehicle can be used by a new owner without re-certification during the two-year validity of the existing Certificate
(d) it needs no further certification unless notifiable alterations are made to its structure

954. It is a legal requirement that vehicles used for international road haulage operations under the TIR Convention must:

(a) display blue and white TIR plates at the front and rear
(b) be certified as meeting the requirements of ADR
(c) display an orange reflex reflecting marker plate at the rear
(d) be certified as meeting the maintenance requirements of the Geneva Convention

955. A 14-volet TIR carnet is valid for the international transportation of goods by road from the UK across a maximum of:

(a) 6 frontiers
(b) 7 frontiers
(c) 10 frontiers
(d) 14 frontiers

956. A vehicle which has a TIR Certificate of Approval:

(a) can be used on international journeys within the EC without a valid TIR carnet
(b) must not be used on journeys to EC member states unless a valid TIR carnet is carried
(c) may not be used on any international journey without a valid TIR carnet
(d) must display blue on white TIR plates at all times

957. Which of the following organisations act as a guarantor for TIR purposes and from which an operator would obtain a TIR carnet?

(a) the London Chamber of Commerce
(b) the DTp through local Traffic Area offices
(c) the Freight Transport Association
(d) the International Road Freight Office

958. TIR Certificates of Approval for goods vehicles are issued by the Department of Transport on behalf of:

(a) the European Customs Union (ECU)
(b) the RHA and FTA
(c) the International Road Transport Union (IRU)
(d) the European Council of Ministers of Transport (ECMT)

959. An ATA carnet is used for:

(a) the temporary importation of goods
(b) the temporary importation of vehicles/trailers
(c) transit of goods on road/rail systems
(d) establishing insurance liability for international loads

960. ATA carnets permit temporary importation of goods without payment of Customs duties or deposits and are applicable:

(a) only to accompanied goods
(b) only to unaccompanied goods
(c) to both accompanied and unaccompanied goods
(d) when permanent import of goods is required

961. The ATA carnet scheme is accepted in which of the following countries?

(a) USSR
(b) Latvia
(c) Turkey
(d) East Germany

962. ATA carnets may be obtained from which of the following organisations?

(a) Chambers of Commerce in main cities
(b) the RHA/FTA
(c) the International Road Freight Office
(d) the Department of Trade and Industry

963. For which of the following countries would it not be necessary to produce a separate certificate of origin for the goods?

(a) Turkey
(b) Yugoslavia
(c) Greece
(d) United Arab Emirates

964. A Bill of Lading is a document used:

(a) to confirm that goods have been loaded on a ship
(b) as a legal receipt for goods received for shipment
(c) to confirm that a ship is loaded to capacity and is ready to sail
(d) to show that goods are at the dockside ready for loading

965. An invoice approved by a representative of the country to which goods are being consigned is called:

(a) a Bill of Lading
(b) a certified invoice
(c) a house bill
(d) a consular invoice

966. One of the main purposes for which consular invoices are required is to control:

(a) illegal entry of import goods
(b) illegal transfer of exchange currencies
(c) payment of Customs duties
(d) the influx of pornographic and illicit goods

967. SITPRO is concerned with:

(a) simplifying documents and procedures in international trade
(b) the quota system for allocating international road haulage permits

(c) the international system for taxation of road vehicles
(d) international Customs procedures for trade within the EC

968. The SITPRO system provides exporters with:

(a) simplified Customs clearance at national frontiers
(b) automatic pre-entry at Customs offices of departure
(c) aligned documentation
(d) bonds against payment or deposits of Customs duty

969. What document used in export trade is looked upon as a legal receipt for goods received for shipment or for goods shipped?

(a) a Bill of Lading
(b) a consular invoice
(c) a CMR consignment note
(d) an ATA carnet

970. The forked (bracket) tariff scheme is operated to ensure that:

(a) haulage operations between EC member states are charged at rates within laid down maximum and minimum levels
(b) hauliers throughout the Community charge the same haulage rates for the same type of work
(c) haulage rates charged for the carriage of goods by road within the EC do not undercut the equivalent railway rate for the distance
(d) haulage rates charged for intra-Community work do not breach the EC's fair competition rules

971. Forked (bracket) tariff rules lay down maximum and minimum rates:

(a) for the carriage of goods within individual EC member states
(b) for the carriage of goods by road between EC member states

(c) for the taxation of international haulage vehicles across the Community
(d) chargeable on imports received by road into EC member states

972. Although not yet operational in the UK, the system of reference tariffs:

(a) is mandatory in all EC member states
(b) is published for the guidance of hauliers wishing to know what rates to charge
(c) is mandatory only in EC member states which have implemented them
(d) will only become mandatory if haulage associations approve them

973. Where EC member states have instituted a system of forked (bracket) tariffs, the regulations do not apply to the carriage of goods under a distance of:

(a) 25 kilometres
(b) 50 kilometres
(c) 100 kilometres
(d) 150 kilometres

974. Bracket tariffs cover a range of prices with a bracket spread between the minimum and maximum rates no greater than:

(a) 10 per cent
(b) 13 per cent
(c) 23 per cent
(d) 33 per cent

975. When fluctuating exchange rates result in the French franc being raised in relation to sterling, expenses for a British haulier in France will be:

(a) lower
(b) the same
(c) higher

976. If France devalues the franc by 10 per cent this will result in:

(a) reduced costs for UK hauliers in France
(b) increased costs for UK hauliers in France
(c) unchanged costs for UK hauliers in France

977. If the French franc is weak in relation to sterling a UK driver buying fuel in France would:

(a) find the cost to be less in sterling
(b) find the cost to be more in sterling
(c) notice no difference in costs between France and the UK
(d) be better advised to pay for the fuel in francs

978. If a bulk road tanker carries hazardous substances between the UK and West Germany what regulations apply?

(a) British hazardous goods regulations
(b) ATP Convention rules
(c) AGR Convention rules
(d) ADR and IMDG blue book rules

979. Which of the following countries bans the carriage of dangerous goods on its roads during all or part of the weekend?

(a) Norway
(b) France
(c) Portugal
(d) Belgium

980. A European Accident Statement:

(a) is required by the gendarmerie of EC states in which a road accident occurs
(b) assists insurance companies to deal more efficiently with claims arising from motor accidents in Europe
(c) must be completed by all UK drivers involved in accidents abroad
(d) ensures that blame for road accidents in Europe can be readily established

981. The AGR convention establishes:

(a) a European system for numbering road networks
(b) a system for control of the carriage of hazardous goods
(c) standard conditions of carriage for international journeys
(d) a system for controlling bilateral road haulage permit quotas

982. A UK haulier taking an abnormal indivisible load to France will need to seek authority from:

(a) French Customs authorities
(b) the French Department of Transport, Paris
(c) the French Embassy in London
(d) the police for each region in France through which the load will pass

983. Which of the following countries imposes a Sunday driving ban on goods vehicles over 6 tonnes?

(a) Austria
(b) West Germany
(c) Spain
(d) France

984. Which of the following countries imposes a ban on the movement of goods vehicles on their roads from noon Saturday to midnight Sunday?

(a) Denmark
(b) France
(c) Austria
(d) Italy

985. Which of the following countries bans goods vehicles over 7.5 tonnes laden weight from using motorways between 07.00 hrs on Saturday and 22.00 hrs on Sunday during the months of June and September?

(a) West Germany
(b) Yugoslavia
(c) Austria
(d) Greece

986. Which of the following countries bans the transit of heavy goods vehicles on Sunday?

(a) Norway
(b) Switzerland
(c) Yugoslavia
(d) East Germany

987. It is compulsory for goods vehicles over 3.5 tonnes to carry wheel chocks in Austria.

(a) True
(b) False

988. The height of a vehicle and its load travelling through the Netherlands and West Germany should not exceed:

(a) 3.5 metres
(b) 4 metres
(c) 4.2 metres
(d) 4.5 metres

989. It is a requirement that British vehicles travelling through France must comply with French lighting regulations for headlights to be yellow.

(a) True
(b) False

990. The current maximum length permitted for a road train in Europe is:

(a) 15.5 metres
(b) 16.5 metres
(c) 18 metres
(d) 18.2 metres

991. The maximum permitted length for a UK semi-trailer used on international journeys prior to 1 January 1990 was:

(a) 15.5 metres
(b) 12.2 metres
(c) any length provided that the total vehicle length did not exceed 15.5m
(d) any length provided that the load carrying space did not exceed 12.2m

992. The Freight Containers (Safety Convention) Regulations 1984 require safety approval plates for freight containers to be issued by:

(a) the Health and Safety Executive (or a body appointed by the HSE)
(b) the Freight Transport Association
(c) Department of Transport Goods Vehicle Test Stations
(d) the British Safety Council

993. The principal advantage of using the 'Kangourou' road-rail system for international journeys through France is that it:

(a) dispenses with the need for TIR carnets
(b) dispenses with the need to operate under the CMR convention
(c) avoids the need for payment of deposits against Customs duties
(d) overcomes shortages in bilateral quota permits

994. The French Railways (SNCF) 'Kangourou' road-rail system which exempts hauliers from the need for a permit to transit France:

(a) must be used for both outward and return journeys
(b) may be used for the outward journey only
(c) may be used for the return journey only
(d) applies only for traffic passing through one-way to West Germany

995. Road vehicles transported for part of their journey by the French (SNCF) or West German (DB) railway systems must carry:

(a) a bilateral quota road haulage permit
(b) a road-rail certificate
(c) an ECMT road haulage permit
(d) a carnet de passage en douane

996. Road-rail certificates for international road haulage journeys to or in transit through France can be obtained from:

(a) French Railways (SNCF) in London
(b) British Rail International Shipping office

(c) the International Road Freight Office
(d) the Franco-British Chamber of Commerce

997. The road-rail system operated by West German Railways (DB) which enables vehicles to transit the state without a road haulage permit can be used for:

(a) complete vehicles only
(b) unaccompanied trailers only
(c) accompanied vehicles and unaccompanied trailers
(d) accompanied trailers and semi-trailers only

998. Road-rail certificates must be stamped by rail authorities as proof that:

(a) the vehicle/trailer has been carried on the train
(b) the necessary Customs clearances have been obtained en route
(c) an ATA carnet exists for temporary importation of the vehicle
(d) the vehicle/trailer and load are fully insured for CMR liabilities

999. The system whereby a number of small consignments are consolidated into a unit load is called:

(a) cabotage
(b) freight forwarding
(c) groupage
(d) containerisation

1000. Which of the following organisations provides a groupage service?

(a) a freight forwarder
(b) the Freight Transport Association
(c) the Road Haulage Association
(d) the International Road Transport Union (IRU)

1001. Under which international convention are UK vehicles travelling abroad required to carry independently-powered flashing lights?

(a) AETR convention
(b) CMR convention

(c) ADR convention
(d) AGR convention

7: Typical Questions – Northern Ireland Goods National Examination

Module A

1. Unless lower general speed limits are in force, or a vehicle is restricted to a lower limit, on single carriageway restricted roads the speed limit is:
   (a) 30mph
   (b) 40mph
   (c) 60mph
   (d) 70mph

2. An articulated goods vehicle not exceeding 7.5 tonnes maximum laden weight may be driven on a de-restricted dual carriageway other than a motorway in Northern Ireland at a maximum speed of:
   (a) 40mph
   (b) 50mph
   (c) 60mph
   (d) 70mph

3. Every goods vehicle to which a trailer is attached must have its front and rear position lights illuminated during the hours of darkness:
   (a) if the unladen weight of the vehicle exceeds 1,525 kg
   (b) when parked within 15 metres of a road junction on either side
   (c) when parked on a restricted speed road
   (d) when parked on any road at night

4. A driver disqualified from driving by the court for 3 years can apply to have the disqualification removed after a period of:

(a) 1 year
(b) 15 months
(c) 18 months
(d) 2 years

5. A haulier contracts the maintenance of his vehicle to a garage. If the vehicle is involved in an accident because it is unfit as a result of the carelessness of an employee of the garage, who is responsible in law for the defective state of the vehicle?

(a) the haulier as the user of the vehicle
(b) the garage because it contracts to do the maintenance
(c) the garage employee for negligence in carrying out the work
(d) both haulier and garage because each is party to the contract

6. Which of the following would be classed as a source of long-term funds for a haulage company?

(a) factoring of its invoices
(b) an issue of ordinary shares to increase its share capital
(c) a bank overdraft
(d) taking trade credit

7. A firm's annual profit and loss account shows:

(a) the success or otherwise of the firm's operations for the year
(b) its outstanding liabilities
(c) its cash position
(d) the value of its assets

8. A firm's balance sheet is a financial statement at a given date showing:

(a) the gross profit made during the past 12 months
(b) the value of the firm's assets and liabilities
(c) the turnover of the business for the past 12 months
(d) the direct and indirect costs of operating the business for the past year

9. **Total capital employed in a business is the sum of:**

   (a) its issued share capital and its reserves of cash
   (b) its issued share capital, reserves of cash and current assets
   (c) its issued share capital, reserves of cash and long-term loans
   (d) its issued share capital, reserves of cash and trade creditors

10. **A financial statement prepared to show the difference between anticipated receipts and payments over a period of time is called:**

    (a) a cash budget
    (b) a statement of account
    (c) a cash analysis statement
    (d) a cash control statement

11. **If a firm makes a net profit of £40,000 and has £100,000 capital employed the return on capital is:**

    (a) £60,000
    (b) £140,000
    (c) 40 per cent
    (d) 60 per cent

12. **Cash flow will normally be improved within a business by offering:**

    (a) smaller cash discounts to customers
    (b) larger cash discounts to customers
    (c) smaller trade discounts to customers
    (d) credit sale facilities to customers

13. **A cash discount is normally allowed to a purchaser of goods who:**

    (a) pays his account promptly
    (b) has bought the goods on a 'sale or return' basis
    (c) has bought goods for resale
    (d) is required to pay in advance for the goods

14. **If an approximate price for a job is given to a customer in advance this is:**

(a) a statement
(b) an estimate
(c) a quotation
(d) a pro forma

15. A debit note would be issued by a firm to:
(a) instruct its bankers to debit an amount owed to a supplier
(b) summarise a customer's total indebtedness
(c) refund money owed to a customer
(d) notify a customer of an additional charge

16. A credit note may be issued to:
(a) pay a specific debt
(b) correct an overcharge on an invoice
(c) inform a customer of his total indebtedness at a particular date
(d) correct an undercharge on an invoice

17. A road haulier should plan his anticipated future purchases:
(a) for those periods when cash outflow is high
(b) for those periods when cash inflow is low
(c) for those periods when cash inflow is high
(d) for those periods when cash outflow is low

18. The method by which debtors can pay amounts owed directly into a bank account rather than by sending a cheque is called:
(a) direct debit
(b) credit transfer
(c) standing order
(d) factoring

19. Which of the following is the safest type of cheque?
(a) one that is ante-dated
(b) a bearer cheque
(c) an open cheque
(d) a banker's draft

20. What type of insurance would an employer take out as cover against injuries caused to passers-by by his vehicle shedding an insecure load?

(a) comprehensive
(b) third party
(c) public liability
(d) employers' liability

21. The Carriage of Goods by Road Act 1965 relates to which of the following types of insurance?

(a) fleet cover
(b) cover against CMR liabilities
(c) third-party motor vehicle cover
(d) goods in transit

22. A contract for the carriage of goods by road:

(a) must be in writing
(b) must be in writing if carriage charges are more than a certain value
(c) must be confirmed in writing if made verbally
(d) can be made verbally or in writing

23. The liability of a private carrier for loss of goods carried on behalf of customers is:

(a) unlimited
(b) unlimited in accordance with quoted conditions of carriage
(c) restricted to the limit set out in its conditions of carriage
(d) limited to a maximum value of £800 per tonne

24. An agent who takes a bribe can:

(a) only be dismissed with reasonable notice from his principal
(b) be dismissed without notice but is not criminally liable
(c) be dismissed without notice and held criminally responsible
(d) only be dismissed if he refused to reimburse his principal with a sum equivalent to the amount of the bribe

25. A main contractor sub-contracting work to a third person:

(a) remains fully liable to the customer for the fulfilment of the contract
(b) is not liable to the client for the fulfilment of the contract
(c) is not liable if the sub-contractor undertakes to accept full responsibility for the fulfilment of the contract
(d) is not liable for the fulfilment of the contract if the sub-contract is made in writing

26. The occupier of premises owes a common duty of care towards:

(a) employees only
(b) visitors only
(c) employees and visitors
(d) employees, visitors and unauthorised trespassers

27. The initial letters PLC after a firm's name signify that the business is a:

(a) public limited company
(b) private limited company
(c) public limited carrier
(d) private limited carrier

28. If creditors voluntarily wind up a limited company, the liquidator is appointed by:

(a) the Registrar of Companies
(b) the courts
(c) the creditors
(d) the company itself

29. An employee who has worked for the same employer for 7 years is entitled to:

(a) 2 weeks' notice
(b) 7 weeks' notice
(c) 2 months' notice
(d) 3 months' notice

30. If an employer fails to pay all or part of the guarantee pay owed to an employee because he cannot find work

for him, the employee has a statutory right to lodge a complaint with:

(a) the Department of Economic Development
(b) an industrial tribunal
(c) a magistrates' court
(d) his own trade union

31. Which of the following are entitled to redundancy payments?

(a) a 17 year old apprentice
(b) a 67 year old mechanic
(c) an office worker who has worked for 26 hours a week for 9 years
(d) a self-employed lorry driver

32. Time off work with pay is allowed under employment protection legislation to:

(a) an employee to attend a local authority meeting in his capacity as a councillor
(b) an employee to attend a magistrates' court in his capacity as a Justice of the Peace
(c) a trade union member to attend a shop stewards' training course
(d) an ordinary trade union member to attend a union meeting

33. A driver aged 47 has been with his employer since he was 16. A recession forces the firm to close down and he is made redundant. Under redundancy pay legislation he will be entitled to a redundancy payment based on:

(a) his last 20 complete years' service with the company
(b) 27 complete years' service with the company
(c) 29 complete years' service with the company
(d) 31 complete years' service with the company

34. Which of the following items of information must legally be included in the written statement of the main terms of employment that employers are obliged to

give to employees within 13 weeks of commencing employment?

(a) travelling allowances claimable
(b) place of work
(c) subsistence allowances claimable
(d) sick pay arrangements

35. The Fair Employment (Northern Ireland) Act 1989 deals with matters of:

(a) equal pay
(b) unfair dismissal
(c) sex discrimination
(d) political discrimination

36. If a Health and Safety inspector issues an employer with an improvement notice the system of work to which it relates:

(a) must cease immediately until the required improvements are made
(b) must cease immediately unless the employer appeals against the notice
(c) may continue provided that the required improvements are made within the specified time limit
(d) may continue provided that the firm's safety representatives agree

37. If a Health and Safety inspector issues an employer with a prohibition notice the system of work to which it relates:

(a) may continue in operation provided that the required improvements are made within the specified time limit
(b) must cease immediately until the required improvements are made
(c) may continue in operation only provided that the firm's safety representative agrees
(d) must cease immediately unless the employer appeals against the notice

38. The aim of the Equal Pay Act (NI) 1970 is to end the inequality between men and women in relation to their:

(a) pension benefits
(b) opportunities for promotion
(c) terms and conditions of employment
(d) pay compared with workers in other firms

39. Under sex discrimination law, which of the following advertisements placed by a company with 20 employees would be classed as legally acceptable?

(a) male washroom attendant required
(b) tea lady required
(c) male road haulage driver required
(d) female receptionist required

40. If a claim by a woman for equal terms and conditions of employment with her male colleague is not granted by her employer the matter can be referred for settlement to:

(a) an industrial training board
(b) the Department of the Environment
(c) an industrial court
(d) an industrial tribunal

Module B

41. A 'week' as defined in EC drivers' hours regulation 3820/85 is:

(a) a fixed period from 00.00 hours Sunday to 24.00 hours Saturday
(b) a fixed period from 00.00 hours Monday to 24.00 hours Sunday
(c) any 7-day period agreed by the Licensing Authority
(d) any rolling period of 7 consecutive days

42. Under EC regulation 3820/85 the normal daily driving period of 9 hours may be increased twice in any one week to:

(a) 9.5 hours
(b) 10 hours
(c) 11 hours

(d) 12 hours

43. During the past week an HGV driver has spent 34 hours driving. Under EC drivers' hours regulations, for what period is he allowed to drive during the current week?

(a) 56 hours
(b) 48 hours
(c) 59 hours
(d) 60 hours

44. It is permissible under EC regulation 3820/85 for a driver to split up a non-reduced daily rest period into 2 or 3 separate periods during the 24 hours. When split in this manner the minimum total daily rest period must be:

(a) 10 hours
(b) 11 hours
(c) 12 hours
(d) 15 hours

45. A driver of a goods vehicle plated at 12 tonnes maximum weight operating in Northern Ireland under EC drivers' hours regulations is limited to:

(a) 8 hours driving per day and 12 hours twice in the week
(b) 8 hours driving per day and 11 hours twice in the week
(c) 9 hours driving per day and 10 hours twice in the week
(d) 11 hours driving per day and 9 hours twice in the week

46. A driver of a goods vehicle who is subject to the EC drivers' hours rules stops for a break after driving continuously for 2 hours. What is the minimum break he may take for it to be recognised as an official break?

(a) 5 minutes
(b) 15 minutes
(c) 20 minutes

(d) 45 minutes

47. A driver of a heavy goods vehicle with a permissible maximum weight of 20 tonnes, operating under EC drivers' hours regulations, is limited to a maximum weekly driving time of:

(a) 58 hours
(b) 54 hours
(c) 56 hours
(d) 60 hours

48. A driver of a heavy goods vehicle with a permissible maximum weight of 15 tonnes commences a journey at 10am. At 11.30am he takes a break of 20 minutes and at 1.20pm he takes a further break from driving of 15 minutes. If he has a further break from driving at 3.05pm, what is the minimum length of break he must take at that time to satisfy the law?

(a) 10 minutes
(b) 15 minutes
(c) 30 minutes
(d) 45 minutes

49. EC regulations require that unless otherwise exempt all goods vehicles exceeding 3.5 tonnes gross weight must be fitted with an approved tachograph. When calculating the gross weight of the vehicle for this purpose, the weight of any goods-carrying trailer drawn:

(a) must always be included
(b) is only included if the weight of the trailer exceeds 3.5 tonnes
(c) is never included
(d) is only included if the unladen weight of the trailer exceeds 1,020kg

50. Which of the following vehicles must be fitted with a tachograph to record drivers' hours on EC journeys?

(a) vehicles used solely for transporting animal carcasses not intended for human consumption

(b) specialised breakdown vehicles
(c) a vehicle with a permissible maximum weight of 12 tonnes used for milk collection from farms
(d) a goods vehicle and trailer with a permissible maximum weight of 5 tonnes used to transport commercial goods

51. Calibration and sealing of tachographs to comply with EC regulations can only be carried out at:

(a) the vehicle owner's premises
(b) a DoE approved tachograph centre
(c) the vehicle manufacturer's premises
(d) the tachograph manufacturer's premises

52. If a driver changes during a period of duty from one vehicle to another, both of which are fitted with the same kind of tachograph, he must take the tachograph chart from the first vehicle with him and:

(a) insert the original chart from the first vehicle into the instrument in the second vehicle
(b) insert a new chart into the instrument in the second vehicle
(c) record in an individual control book the necessary information relating to the time spent with the second vehicle
(d) record on a temporary sheet the necessary information relating to the time spent with the second vehicle

53. If examination of the speed recordings on a tachograph chart shows many high peaks and troughs very close together this indicates:

(a) normal driving of an acceptable standard
(b) normal driving but needing some improvement
(c) poor and uneconomic driving
(d) good and economic driving

54. Which of the following persons has legal authority to examine drivers' records?

(a) a traffic warden

(b) a Customs and Excise officer
(c) a police constable
(d) a Health and Safety inspector

55. The minimum age at which a person can hold a full HGV Class 2 or 3 driving licence in Northern Ireland is:

(a) 17 years
(b) 18 years
(c) 20 years
(d) 21 years

56. The Department of the Environment in Northern Ireland has the power to suspend or revoke an HGV driver's licence on the grounds of:

(a) physical disability
(b) being drunk and disorderly in a public bar
(c) misconduct unconnected with driving the vehicle
(d) failing to properly complete his tachograph records

57. Applicants for an HGV driving licence must declare any convictions for driving under the influence of alcohol or drugs during the previous:

(a) 3 years
(b) 5 years
(c) 7 years
(d) 10 years

58. If a haulage company operates articulated vehicles with tractive units over 2 tonnes unladen, it would need to employ drivers with HGV driving licences of:

(a) Class 1
(b) Class 2
(c) Class 2A
(d) Class 3

59. A driver who is involved in a road accident in which his vehicle collides with a cow can find nobody to whom he can give particulars at the time so he must report the accident to the police:

(a) only if the cow is seriously injured
(b) as soon as is reasonably practicable and in any case within 24 hours
(c) within 5 days at a police station near to where the accident occured
(d) within 7 days at any police station

60. The vehicle in which a test applicant takes the HGV driving test:

(a) may be over 7.5 tonnes permissible maximum weight
(b) may be either laden or unladen
(c) must be laden
(d) must be unladen

61. If approved by the Secretary of State a fleet operator may cover his own third-party motor insurance risks provided he deposits sufficient security with:

(a) the Accountant General of the Supreme Court of NI
(b) the NI Road Transport Industry Training Board
(c) the NI Department of the Environment
(d) the Motor Insurers' Bureau

62. Invalidation of a motor insurance policy means that the insurers will:

(a) increase premiums at the next renewal date
(b) refuse to honour the agreement in the event of claims arising
(c) always refuse to renew the policy when it falls due
(d) disclaim liability if the insured operates his vehicles outside the terms of the policy

63. The function of an insurance certificate is to:

(a) provide proof that the driver is not disqualified from driving
(b) show the estimated insurance value of a motor vehicle
(c) provide proof that the driver has paid his insurance premiums

(d) provide evidence that the vehicle is legally insured

64. If a motor vehicle is insured in respect of third-party risks when used for domestic and pleasure purposes only, the insurance cover will be invalidated if the owner:

(a) carries goods in the vehicle for hire and reward
(b) carries tools in the vehicle for use in connection with his employment
(c) carries unauthorised passengers
(d) picks up hitch-hikers

65. An HGV driver who is asked to produce his certificate of motor insurance at an RUC station:

(a) must advise his insurers that he has been asked to produce it
(b) must produce the certificate in person
(c) may produce it himself or have another person do so for him
(d) must produce it in person accompanied by his employer

66. A haulier who has inadvertently failed to renew his third-party insurance is involved in an accident in which a pedestrian is badly injured due to the driver's negligence. The injured person can claim compensation through:

(a) the Motor Insurers' Bureau
(b) his own motor insurance company
(c) the Road Haulage Association
(d) a special government fund

67. A certificate of motor insurance must contain details of:

(a) the premiums paid on the policy
(b) the persons authorised to drive vehicles covered by the policy
(c) whether or not the vehicles have been purchased under a hire purchase agreement
(d) the amount of licence excise duty paid on motor vehicles covered by the policy

68. **If a load shifts or fall from a goods vehicle, who is liable to prosecution for having an insecure load?**
    (a) the driver only
    (b) the haulier only
    (c) both the haulier and the driver
    (d) the person who loaded the vehicle

69. **The driver of a vehicle carrying dangerous goods must be provided with full information about the identity of the substance, the dangers which could arise from it and emergency action to be taken. This information:**
    (a) must be given both orally and in writing
    (b) can be given orally
    (c) must be given in writing
    (d) can be given orally or in writing

70. **Records covering the carriage of livestock by road must be retained at the vehicle owner's premises for a minimum period of:**
    (a) 3 months
    (b) 4 months
    (c) 6 months
    (d) 12 months

71. **When an abnormal indivisible load has to be transported in NI by road the police must be given at least 2 days' clear notice if the gross weight of the vehicle and load exceeds:**
    (a) 24,390 kilograms
    (b) 25,720 kilograms
    (c) 45,720 kilograms
    (d) 76,200 kilograms

72. **Under UK regulations an attendant must be carried on a vehicle having a forward projection of:**
    (a) 1.07 metres
    (b) 1.50 metres
    (c) 1.75 metres
    (d) 2.00 metres

73. **The weight of a vehicle in a road-going condition, inclusive of oil, water and fuel but without the driver and load, is defined as the:**

(a) kerb weight
(b) tare weight
(c) gross vehicle weight
(d) gross train weight

74. A heavy goods vehicle is a large goods vehicle constructed or adapted to carry or haul goods and having a permissible maximum weight exceeding:

(a) 2.0 tonnes
(b) 3.5 tonnes
(c) 6.0 tonnes
(d) 7.5 tonnes

75. The maximum permissible weight for a rigid vehicle having two axles more than 2.65 metres apart is:

(a) 14,230 kilograms
(b) 15,250 kilograms
(c) 16,260 kilograms
(d) 18,290 kilograms

76. The maximum legal height of the structure of a goods vehicle in NI is:

(a) 3.8 metres
(b) 4 metres
(c) 4.2 metres
(d) 5 metres

77. What is the maximum height limit allowable for an articulated vehicle having a total laden weight exceeding 32,520kg, the semi-trailer of which has a gross weight exceeding 26,000kg?

(a) 4 metres
(b) 4.2 metres
(c) 4.3 metres
(d) 4.5 metres

78. The overhang on a goods vehicle must not exceed:

(a) 30 per cent of the wheelbase
(b) 40 per cent of the wheelbase
(c) 50 per cent of the wheelbase

(d) 60 per cent of the wheelbase

79. The overhang on a heavy motor vehicle with twin rear axles is measured from a point:

(a) midway between the two rear axles
(b) 100mm behind the midway point between the two rear axles
(c) 110mm behind the midway point between the two rear axles
(d) 100mm ahead of the midway point between the two rear axles

80. One of the factors influencing permitted gross vehicle weight is axle spread. On a rigid 8-wheeled vehicle this is taken to be the distance between:

(a) the foremost and rearmost axles
(b) the rearmost front axle and the foremost rear axle
(c) the two rear axles
(d) the rearmost front axle and the rearmost rear axle

81. If a new heavy goods vehicle has a main braking system with an efficiency of 50 per cent and a secondary braking system of 20 per cent efficiency, the law is satisfied in respect of:

(a) both the main and secondary braking systems
(b) the main braking system only
(c) neither of the two braking systems
(d) the secondary braking system only

82. If a solid towbar is not employed, the nearest point between two vehicles joined by a towrope must not exceed:

(a) 1.5 metres
(b) 2.5 metres
(c) 3.5 metres
(d) 4.5 metres

83. The minimum length in law for a rigid towbar is:

(a) not specified
(b) 1.5 metres

(c) 3.5 metres
(d) 4.5 metres

84. Tyres must not be used on goods vehicles if they have a cut which reaches the body cords or is greater in length than:

(a) 10mm or 5 per cent of the section width of the tyre
(b) 15mm or 5 per cent of the section width of the tyre
(c) 20mm or 5 per cent of the section width of the tyre
(d) 25mm or 10 per cent of the section width of the tyre

85. Re-cut tyres must not be used on goods vehicles under 2,540 kg unladen weight unless the wheel rim diameter is at least:

(a) 225mm
(b) 305mm
(c) 355mm
(d) 405mm

86. Front position lamps (other than those with approval marks) fitted to goods vehicles must have a minimum intensity:

(a) to ensure visibility from a reasonable distance
(b) of 7 watts
(c) of 8 watts
(d) of 10 watts

87. An immediate prohibition notice issued by a motor vehicle examiner relates to:

(a) merely the carriage of goods on the vehicle
(b) the use of the vehicle for specific purposes
(c) the use of the vehicle on the road for any purpose
(d) the use of the vehicle above a specified maximum speed

88. For the purpose of ensuring that goods vehicles are being maintained in a fit and serviceable condition a DoE inspector can test a vehicle:

(a) on the road or at the operator's premises

(b) only at a goods vehicle testing centre
(c) only at the roadside
(d) only at the operator's premises

89. Which of the following documents must be presented at the time a goods vehicle is being examined at a DoE vehicle inspection centre in connection with the granting of a Goods Vehicle Certificate?

(a) operator's licence
(b) vehicle registration book
(c) certificate of professional competence
(d) motor insurance certificate

90. A road freight operator with a large fleet of vehicles has held a maximum of 60 vehicle licences during the last 3 years. The DoE may revoke or suspend his operator's licence if during that period he has had:

(a) 6 vehicle licences revoked or suspended
(b) 10 vehicle licences revoked or suspended
(c) 4 vehicle licences revoked or suspended
(d) 3 vehicle licences revoked or suspended

91. When deciding whether or not an applicant for a road freight operator's licence is of good repute the DoE will take into account:

(a) all offences recorded against the applicant during the previous 5 years
(b) only road traffic offences recorded against the applicant during the previous 5 years
(c) only road traffic offences involving licence endorsement recorded against the applicant during the previous 5 years
(d) only road traffic offences recorded against the applicant during the previous 3 years

92. An operator whose transport manager is named as the person holding the CPC has his vehicle maintained by a local garage. Who is legally responsible if appropriate standards of maintenance and relevant records are not maintained?

(a) the garage owner and transport manager
(b) the transport manager
(c) the local garage owner
(d) the operator

93. A road freight operator's licence is:

(a) automatically transferred to the new owner indefinitely
(b) transferred only until due for renewal at the end of the 12-month currency period
(c) only transferable with the previous owner's consent
(d) not transferable and a new licence must be applied for

94. An application for a road freight operator's licence must state:

(a) the number of vehicles proposed to be operated
(b) the unladen weights of the vehicles to be operated
(c) the types of vehicle proposed to be operated
(d) the goods vehicle certificate numbers for the vehicles

95. Which of the following would be classed as a road haulier's operating centre?

(a) the address of the firm's registered office
(b) the garage where the vehicles are maintained
(c) the depot where the vehicles are parked when not in use
(d) the operator's home address

96. A road haulage company's costs include the following items:

tyres	£3,000
rent	£1,000
drivers' basic wages	£16,000
depreciation	£7,000
repairs	£6,000

what would the variable costs amount to?

(a) £27,000

(b) £17,000
(c) £10,000
(d) £9,000

97. A vehicle has 20 gallons of fuel in its tank at the start of a journey. After covering 80 miles there are 12 gallons remaining. What is the average fuel consumption of the vehicle?

(a) 8mpg
(b) 10mpg
(c) 12mpg
(d) 20mpg

98. A vehicle costing £10,000 is estimated to have a useful life of 5 years and a scrap value of £1,000. Using the straight-line method of calculating depreciation, what is the annual depreciation?

(a) £9,000
(b) £5,000
(c) £2,000
(d) £1,800

99. Vehicle excise duty (VED) on a 5-tonne goods vehicle is assessed on the vehicle's:

(a) unladen weight only
(b) gross weight and the number of axles
(c) unladen weight and the number of axles
(d) gross or train weight

100. A groupage operator is a firm which

(a) hires vehicle operators when their own fleets are fully used
(b) delivers goods which a principal contractor has been unable to handle
(c) consolidates individual consignments into unit loads to fill vehicles and containers
(d) arranges for groups of goods vehicles to be sent for plating and testing

Note

Northern Ireland examination candidates are advised that only a limited number of the questions in the NI

examination papers differ from the UK equivalent, so for the most part they will be perfectly safe to study the majority of the mainland syllabus and test themselves on the other typical questions comprising the main part of this book.

8: Answers – National Modules A and B, International Module D, Northern Ireland Modules A and B

National Module A

Q	A	Q	A	Q	A
1	*d*	30	*b*	59	*c*
2	*b*	31	*a*	60	*a*
3	*d*	32	*d*	61	*d*
4	*c*	33	*d*	62	*a*
5	*a*	34	*d*	63	*a*
6	*b*	35	*d*	64	*a*
7	*d*	36	*c*	65	*d*
8	*a*	37	*b*	66	*b*
9	*b*	38	*c*	67	*d*
10	*b*	39	*c*	68	*c*
11	*c*	40	*b*	69	*c*
12	*d*	41	*c*	70	*b*
13	*b*	42	*d*	71	*d*
14	*c*	43	*d*	72	*d*
15	*d*	44	*c*	73	*c*
16	*a*	45	*c*	74	*a*
17	*b*	46	*c*	75	*d*
18	*b*	47	*c*	76	*a*
19	*c*	48	*a*	77	*d*
20	*d*	49	*a*	78	*c*
21	*a*	50	*d*	79	*a*
22	*b*	51	*b*	80	*b*
23	*a*	52	*d*	81	*c*
24	*b*	53	*a*	82	*d*
25	*d*	54	*b*	83	*d*
26	*a*	55	*b*	84	*c*
27	*c*	56	*c*	85	*c*
28	*c*	57	*c*	86	*b*
29	*a*	58	*a*	87	*c*

Q	A	Q	A	Q	A
88	b	128	a	168	b
89	a	129	d	169	c
90	a	130	b	170	b
91	b	131	d	171	d
92	b	132	c	172	a
93	b	133	c	173	d
94	b	134	d	174	c
95	b	135	a	175	d
96	c	136	d	176	d
97	c	137	c	177	a
98	b	138	b	178	c
99	b	139	d	179	d
100	d	140	a	180	c
101	a	141	a	181	a
102	a	142	d	182	b
103	a	143	b	183	d
104	d	144	b	184	b
105	a	145	c	185	d
106	d	146	c	186	b
107	a	147	a	187	c
108	a	148	d	188	b
109	d	149	a	189	b
110	a	150	a	190	c
111	a	151	c	191	c
112	c	152	d	192	b
113	c	153	d	193	c
114	c	154	d	194	c
115	c	155	b	195	b
116	d	156	b	196	d
117	b	157	d	197	d
118	d	158	b	198	d
119	a	159	c	199	c
120	d	160	b	200	b
121	a	161	c	201	d
122	d	162	a	202	a
123	d	163	d	203	d
124	d	164	a	204	c
125	d	165	b	205	b
126	c	166	d	206	c
127	a	167	c	207	a

Q	A	Q	A	Q	A
208	*b*	248	*c*	288	*d*
209	*a*	249	*a*	289	*a*
210	*b*	250	*b*	290	*b*
211	*d*	251	*b*	291	*c*
212	*a*	252	*b*	292	*d*
213	*c*	253	*a*	293	*d*
214	*b*	254	*d*	294	*a*
215	*d*	255	*c*	295	*d*
216	*b*	256	*c*	296	*b*
217	*a*	257	*c*	297	*a*
218	*d*	258	*a*	298	*c*
219	*a*	259	*c*	299	*c*
220	*c*	260	*d*	300	*b*
221	*a*	261	*c*	301	*d*
222	*c*	262	*a*	302	*b*
223	*d*	263	*c*	303	*c*
224	*a*	264	*a*	304	*c*
225	*a*	265	*b*	305	*a*
226	*c*	266	*a*	306	*a*
227	*d*	267	*c*	307	*b*
228	*b*	268	*c*	308	*c*
229	*c*	269	*a*	309	*c*
230	*d*	270	*d*	310	*a*
231	*a*	271	*b*	311	*c*
232	*c*	272	*c*	312	*a*
233	*c*	273	*a*	313	*d*
234	*a*	274	*b*	314	*c*
235	*c*	275	*c*	315	*c*
236	*a*	276	*b*	316	*c*
237	*b*	277	*a*	317	*a*
238	*b*	278	*b*	318	*c*
239	*b*	279	*b*	319	*b*
240	*a*	280	*c*	320	*a*
241	*d*	281	*a*	321	*c*
242	*c*	282	*c*	322	*c*
243	*c*	283	*a*	323	*c*
244	*d*	284	*b*	324	*d*
245	*a*	285	*b*	325	*a*
246	*c*	286	*a*	326	*c*
247	*d*	287	*d*	327	*a*

Q	A	Q	A	Q	A
328	c	336	b	344	c
329	d	337	c	345	b
330	c	338	d	346	d
331	d	339	b	347	c
332	d	340	c	348	a
333	c	341	d	349	b
334	c	342	d	350	c
335	d	343	b		

National Module B

Q	A	Q	A	Q	A
351	d	378	a	405	a
352	b	379	d	406	c
353	b	380	c	407	d
354	d	381	c	408	b
355	b	382	b	409	a
356	a	383	d	410	d
357	b	384	b	411	c
358	d	385	d	412	c
359	c	386	c	413	d
360	b	387	c	414	b
361	c	388	b	415	b
362	d	389	c	416	d
363	c	390	b	417	d
364	c	391	d	418	a
365	b	392	a	419	c
366	c	393	b	420	b
367	d	394	c	421	b
368	b	395	a	422	b
369	b	396	c	423	a
370	c	397	a	424	d
371	b	398	d	425	c
372	b	399	c	426	a
373	c	400	d	427	a
374	a	401	a	428	c
375	b	402	c	429	b
376	d	403	a	430	d
377	a	404	a	431	c

Q	A	Q	A	Q	A
432	*a*	472	*d*	512	*b*
433	*c*	473	*b*	513	*d*
434	*c*	474	*b*	514	*b*
435	*b*	475	*b*	515	*d*
436	*b*	476	*c*	516	*a*
437	*a*	477	*a*	517	*a*
438	*a*	478	*c*	518	*a*
439	*a*	479	*a*	519	*a*
440	*b*	480	*d*	520	*b*
441	*c*	481	*d*	521	*b*
442	*a*	482	*a*	522	*c*
443	*a*	483	*a*	523	*a*
444	*c*	484	*a*	524	*d*
445	*d*	485	*a*	525	*d*
446	*a*	486	*d*	526	*b*
447	*c*	487	*d*	527	*b*
448	*d*	488	*d*	528	*a*
449	*a*	489	*a*	529	*b*
450	*d*	490	*c*	530	*d*
451	*a*	491	*b*	531	*b*
452	*d*	492	*c*	532	*a*
453	*d*	493	*c*	533	*c*
454	*b*	494	*b*	534	*a*
455	*a*	495	*b*	535	*d*
456	*d*	496	*c*	536	*a*
457	*c*	497	*a*	537	*b*
458	*c*	498	*c*	538	*d*
459	*a*	499	*a*	539	*a*
460	*b*	500	*c*	540	*a*
461	*d*	501	*b*	541	*a*
462	*d*	502	*c*	542	*c*
463	*b*	503	*a*	543	*b*
464	*a*	504	*d*	544	*d*
465	*d*	505	*c*	545	*d*
466	*d*	506	*d*	546	*c*
467	*d*	507	*c*	547	*b*
468	*c*	508	*c*	548	*d*
469	*c*	509	*d*	549	*c*
470	*c*	510	*d*	550	*d*
471	*b*	511	*d*	551	*b*

Q	A	Q	A	Q	A
552	d	592	b	632	a
553	b	593	b	633	b
554	b	594	c	634	c
555	c	595	a	635	b
556	c	596	c	636	d
557	a	597	c	637	b
558	d	598	b	638	a
559	c	599	d	639	c
560	c	600	a	640	c
561	d	601	c	641	b
562	c	602	a	642	b
563	c	603	d	643	c
564	d	604	a	644	d
565	c	605	c	645	a
566	c	606	a	646	b
567	d	607	d	647	c
568	a	608	a	648	a
569	c	609	d	649	a
570	b	610	a	650	a
571	b	611	a	651	c
572	c	612	c	652	a
573	c	613	d	653	d
574	a	614	d	654	c
575	c	615	c	655	b
576	b	616	d	656	b
577	b	617	c	657	a
578	d	618	c	658	c
579	d	619	c	659	b
580	b	620	a	660	a
581	b	621	c	661	c
582	b	622	c	662	c
583	a	623	d	663	a
584	a	624	b	664	b
585	d	625	a	665	d
586	b	626	a	666	d
587	b	627	d	667	c
588	c	628	b	668	d
589	a	629	d	669	c
590	b	630	c	670	d
591	c	631	d	671	c

Q	A	Q	A	Q	A
672	*c*	712	*b*	752	*c*
673	*d*	713	*a*	753	*d*
674	*b*	714	*a*	754	*d*
675	*d*	715	*b*	755	*a*
676	*a*	716	*d*	756	*b*
677	*a*	717	*c*	757	*c*
678	*d*	718	*c*	758	*b*
679	*a*	719	*c*	759	*a*
680	*c*	720	*d*	760	*d*
681	*a*	721	*c*	761	*b*
682	*b*	722	*c*	762	*d*
683	*b*	723	*d*	763	*c*
684	*b*	724	*d*	764	*b*
685	*b*	725	*d*	765	*a*
686	*b*	726	*c*	766	*b*
687	*d*	727	*c*	767	*a*
688	*d*	728	*d*	768	*c*
689	*c*	729	*c*	769	*b*
690	*c*	730	*c*	770	*d*
691	*d*	731	*a*	771	*d*
692	*b*	732	*b*	772	*c*
693	*c*	733	*b*	773	*a*
694	*c*	734	*d*	774	*a*
695	*a*	735	*d*	775	*b*
696	*a*	736	*d*	776	*c*
697	*a*	737	*b*	777	*d*
698	*d*	738	*b*	778	*b*
699	*b*	739	*c*	779	*a*
700	*a*	740	*c*	780	*a*
701	*b*	741	*d*	781	*d*
702	*a*	742	*a*	782	*b*
703	*d*	743	*b*	783	*b*
704	*d*	744	*c*	784	*b*
705	*a*	745	*b*	785	*b*
706	*d*	746	*c*	786	*b*
707	*a*	747	*d*	787	*c*
708	*b*	748	*d*	788	*c*
709	*b*	749	*d*	789	*a*
710	*d*	750	*a*	790	*b*
711	*b*	751	*c*	791	*a*

Q	A	Q	A	Q	A
792	c	812	a	832	a
793	b	813	d	833	c
794	b	814	d	834	b
795	b	815	b	835	b
796	b	816	a	836	b
797	c	817	a	837	c
798	c	818	c	838	b
799	b	819	a	839	c
800	b	820	c	840	d
801	b	821	c	841	a
802	d	822	c	842	d
803	d	823	d	843	b
804	a	824	b	844	c
805	c	825	c	845	d
806	d	826	a	846	b
807	b	827	b	847	b
808	d	828	a	848	b
809	b	829	a	849	d
810	c	830	b	850	a
811	b	831	a		

International Module D

Q	A	Q	A	Q	A
851	a	866	c	881	c
852	c	867	d	882	b
853	c	868	c	883	a
854	a	869	a	884	b
855	b	870	a	885	d
856	d	871	d	886	d
857	b	872	b	887	b
858	a	873	b	888	b
859	c	874	a	889	a
860	d	875	b	890	d
861	c	876	a	891	a
862	d	877	c	892	a
863	a	878	c	893	a
864	b	879	c	894	b
865	d	880	b	895	c

Q	A	Q	A	Q	A
896	*a*	936	*c*	976	*a*
897	*a*	937	*a*	977	*a*
898	*d*	938	*c*	978	*d*
899	*b*	939	*a*	979	*b*
900	*a*	940	*d*	980	*b*
901	*c*	941	*a*	981	*a*
902	*c*	942	*d*	982	*d*
903	*c*	943	*b*	983	*d*
904	*b*	944	*b*	984	*c*
905	*c*	945	*a*	985	*a*
906	*a*	946	*b*	986	*b*
907	*c*	947	*c*	987	*a*
908	*d*	948	*a*	988	*b*
909	*a*	949	*a*	989	*b*
910	*c*	950	*a*	990	*c*
911	*d*	951	*b*	991	*c*
912	*a*	952	*c*	992	*a*
913	*a*	953	*a*	993	*d*
914	*b*	954	*a*	994	*a*
915	*b*	955	*a*	995	*b*
916	*d*	956	*a*	996	*c*
917	*b*	957	*c*	997	*c*
918	*c*	958	*c*	998	*a*
919	*b*	959	*a*	999	*c*
920	*d*	960	*c*	1000	*a*
921	*a*	961	*c*	1001	*c*
922	*a*	962	*a*		
923	*b*	963	*c*		
924	*d*	964	*b*		
925	*c*	965	*d*		
926	*b*	966	*c*		
927	*d*	967	*a*		
928	*a*	968	*c*		
929	*c*	969	*a*		
930	*a*	970	*a*		
931	*d*	971	*b*		
932	*b*	972	*c*		
933	*d*	973	*b*		
934	*b*	974	*c*		
935	*c*	975	*c*		

Northern Ireland Modules A and B

Q	A	Q	A	Q	A
1	c	35	d	69	c
2	c	36	c	70	a
3	d	37	b	71	d
4	d	38	c	72	d
5	a	39	a	73	a
6	b	40	d	74	d
7	a	41	b	75	c
8	b	42	b	76	c
9	c	43	a	77	b
10	a	44	c	78	d
11	c	45	c	79	c
12	b	46	b	80	a
13	a	47	c	81	b
14	b	48	b	82	d
15	d	49	a	83	a
16	b	50	d	84	d
17	c	51	b	85	d
18	b	52	a	86	a
19	d	53	c	87	c
20	c	54	c	88	a
21	b	55	d	89	b
22	d	56	a	90	a
23	c	57	d	91	a
24	c	58	a	92	d
25	a	59	b	93	d
26	d	60	d	94	a
27	a	61	a	95	c
28	c	62	b	96	d
29	b	63	d	97	b
30	b	64	a	98	d
31	c	65	c	99	d
32	c	66	a	100	c
33	c	67	b		
34	d	68	c		